Jumping for Joy
In the Midst of Sorrow

By Tekoa Manning

ISBN-13: 978-1-7374020-0-8 (It's All About Him, Inc.)

Jumping for Joy In the Midst of Sorrow Copyright 2021
It's All About Him, Inc.

All rights reserved:

No part of this book may be reproduced in any form or by any electronic or mechanical means including information storage and retrieval systems, without permission in writing from the author. The only exception is by a reviewer, who may quote short excerpts in a review. This is a work of non-fiction.

Editor – Jo Fouts Zausch

Cover by Lynette Marie Smith
Graphic Design & Marketing

Picture on Cover by xavierarnau

CONTENTS

INTRODUCTION ....

Joy and Sorrow ....

SECTION #1 ....

    The God Who Sees You ....

PART 1 ....

    Tree of Life 1

PART 2 ....

    Love thyself 11

PART 3 ....

    The tornado of 1974 19

SECTION #2 ....

    Mirrors of Truth ....

PART 1 ....

    Joyful Outcast 31

PART 2 ....

    Suffering Servants 39

PART 3 ....

    Seeing our True Reflection 47

SECTION #3 ....

    Disability or Divine Calling ....

PART 1 ....

    Harriet 57

PART 2 ....

    A Golden Ticket 67

PART 3 ....

    Gobstoppers 81

SECTION # 4 ....

    Joy is Sitting Right Next to Sorrow ....

PART 1 ....

    Hope Deferred 93

PART 2 ....

    Long Suffering 105

PART 3 ....

    Friends That Shine Like the Son 113

SECTION # 5 ....

    Son Flower Seeds ....

PART 1 ....

    The Potter's House 123

PART 2 ....

    Speak Life 137

PART 3 ....

    Light Birthed in Darkness 147

SECTION # 6 ....

    Darkness and Light ....

PART 1 ....

    David Danced 165

PART 2 ....
    Who has a Broken Heart? 177
PART 3 ....
    Joy and Barrenness 185
Blessings 193

INTRODUCTION

Joy and Sorrow

A woman said, "Speak to us of Joy and Sorrow." And he answered: Your joy is your sorrow, unmasked. And the selfsame well from which your laughter rises was oftentimes filled with your tears. And how else can it be? The deeper that sorrow carves into your being, the more joy you can contain.

—Khalil Gibran

At this moment, you may be filled with so much despair that you can scarcely breathe. Things in your life may seem so bleak that to find an ounce of joy would seem unimaginable. David proclaims the Lord keeps track of every tear: "You have taken account of my miseries; Put my tears in Your bottle. Are they not in Your book?" (Psalm 56:8, NASB). My prayer is that laughter rises from tear-filled bottles and that pure joy overtakes you to the point you are jumping and leaping—shouting even.

What do we know about joy--pure joy, not imitation, not a winning lottery ticket-- but joy that comes from a dark place and soothes every ache with ointment? There is a joy that sings like amber sap spilling into tree limbs running down to the roots. The

Psalmist describes trees of the field clapping their hands to welcome the dawn. May your sorrow bring a delightful joy that makes your feet dance. May there be a joyful gladness that infuses your heart until it bursts forth with shouts of joy.

I want to write a book about joy but find no way to write about joy without writing about sorrow, anguish, and pain. The Book of Galatians lists joy next to longsuffering. Is it possible that these two go hand in hand? The fear of emotional suffering often restricts a person's ability to experience joy. After becoming disabled in my late 30s and being declared fully disabled at age 42, I know a bit about pain on a personal level. Pain and suffering do not just affect us; they affect everyone around us. After losing every title that defined me as a person, the Father stripped me bare and took me on a journey of suffering that unleashed so much joy that I would not trade a minute of the pain. Suffering has been my most faithful teacher. Like a recliner soft and worn with age, I have learned much from pain and sorrow. It was on my journey of brokenness that I found gratitude and how to calm and quiet my soul. It was pain, sorrow, and hopelessness that caused me to look up to the heavens and raise my feeble arms in surrender. Like a wild horse needing to be broken, I soon realized I was not in control. The famous poet Robert Browning Hamilton expounds on sorrow.

> *I walked a mile with Pleasure;*
>
> *She chatted all the way;*

But left me none the wiser

For all, she had to say.

I walked a mile with Sorrow;

And ne'er a word said she;

But, oh! The things I learned from her,

When Sorrow walked with me.

Sorrow and pain come in somber colors with blackened curtains that cover windows of opportunity. This weighted down worry and heartache can keep us awake at night. Our insecurities and fears can bow our posture and cause us to lose our voice or refrain from reaching higher levels of intimacy. One morning we wake up feeling like a discarded garment at a rummage sale or a child left alone, abandoned, and unappreciated. The feeling of being invisible in a crowded room, feeling unworthy or unloved, can be excruciating. Loneliness, heartbreak, depression, fears, and yes, a body or mind or both that no longer function as it used to, all these evoke pain. Weary desert travelers' thirst for water and seek bread from the heavens. Their parched souls are crying out for a drop of joy, but just around the bend, with one draw of the curtains, there is light, vision, and new beginnings. With one ladle dipped into our Father's well, there is living water.

How do we make our journey from this mundane existence to heavenly joy? We wrap ourselves in the comfort of His light and His love. We become still from the inside out. We embrace ourselves. Our arms hold our soul, rocking and weeping. We feel every bit of the emptiness — the silence, the shame we have dressed ourselves in while weaving fig leaves and running from reality. Until finally, we open His Word and drink from the wellsprings of life. Then suddenly, He speaks, and we hear Him. It is the loudest voice we have ever heard and also the gentlest, most loving sound ever whispered. His still soft Voice comforts us. He says the same thing He spoke to Adam and Elijah, and many others, "Where are you? What are you doing here, here in this thirsty land?"

> Ho! Everyone who thirsts, come to the waters; And you who have no money come, buy and eat. Come, buy wine and milk. Without money and without cost. Why do you spend money for what is not bread, and your wages for what does not satisfy? Listen carefully to Me, and eat what is good, And delight yourself in abundance.
>
> –Isaiah 55:1-2, NASB

Suddenly joy bubbles forth like a brook. This new joy sings like the birds in spring. It is a joy that dances before the Ark as David did, a joy that causes Miriam to take a tambourine and make sweet melodies. It is the joy that filled Hannah, Sarah, Rebekah, and Rachel's dry, dead wombs. It is a joy that pours over your head like a horn of oil. A joy that causes your feet to tap and your chest to burst, your sleep to not come because you are so overwhelmed by the goodness of the Father of Glory. This is the joy we crave. All the people mentioned above went through profound darkness before they reached the dancing and shouting. Like ours, their stories have sorrow, crushing, pressing, and wineskins filled with tears—wretched darkness so deep, a womb so empty, years of being hunted by enemies, and trials beyond belief, but eventually they sing, dance, and shout with joy.

It is my deepest hope that through the words of this book, you are able to hear His Voice and see your worth. Hold on tight, for all your sorrow and brokenness is doing a greater work unseen to the naked eye. Often our places of mourning and darkness are carving out a place of gratitude and sunlight. Despair and brokenness can be a heavenly tool. Pruning and fiery trials can lead you smack dab into the face of joy. Suffering has divine purpose. Do not look at suffering as punishment. Suffering is often designed by the Holy One to bring about a positive future circumstance. Ego takes a backseat. When David lost his son by Bathsheba, he worshipped. When Job lost all his oxen, servants, and children, he fell prostrate and worshipped. When David was being chased by King Saul, he praised the Holy One, writing some of the most poignant words ever spoken. When Leah was unloved and could not bear children, Adonai opened her womb, and after giving birth to her fourth son, Judah, she praises Adonai. Rachel desperately pleas: 'Give me children, or I shall die! She gives birth to a son and names him Joseph. Joseph not only answers Rachel's cry for life, but goes on to give bread to the hungry so they won't perish. When evil happens to Joseph, he sees with wisdom and says, "As for you (my brothers), you meant evil against me, but God meant it for good in order to bring about this present result, to keep many people alive" (Genesis 50:20, NASB). Author and poet, Mary Oliver said it best when she said, "Someone I loved once gave me a box full of darkness. It took me years to understand that this too, was a gift." Yes, after the smoke clears, if you will continue to lift your feeble arms up in praise, looking to the Author and Finisher of your faith, eventually, you too will see the joy in the most teachable moments of despair, wrapped in darkness that ushers in redemption.

SECTION # 1

The God Who Sees You

The next three devotionals are about loving ourselves and knowing that our Father is in the tiniest, most intricate details.

> *So Hagar gave this name to the LORD who had spoken to her: "You are the God who sees me," for she said, "Here I have seen the One who sees me!"*
>
> *--Genesis 16:13, BSB.*

PART 1

Tree of Life

From the details of my life, it would seem I am the least qualified to write a book about joy. But pure joy can come from ashes. Yes, joy bubbling forth like a fountain comes after the trials, the testing, and great suffering. Joy is mostly misunderstood in western culture. Joy is not a symphony but rather an unusual melody woven together in cords of silver and gold that come forth through a fiery furnace that purifies.

Joy comes to Miriam after her brother Lazarus is sick. Miriam pleads for the Master, Yeshua, to please come to her town and heal her brother. Four days later, her reply is bitter, "You're too late, he is dead." Miriam had hope while her brother still lived, but now her hope is deferred. Our Messiah can bring dead things back to life. Dead relationships, dead businesses, dead ministries, prodigal children, suffering, insanity, all become sane, healed, and whole when Yeshua speaks life over our situations. Can you hear Him saying, "Arise, my daughter, my son, and come forth from the dead?" In the midst of thick darkness and stormy turbulence, when we fear for our lives, our Messiah says, "Peace, be still. Shh, my child."

In 1984, I was a frightened, pregnant teenager. I was over 800 miles away from home on a military base in North Carolina. I had my firstborn a month early and was in intense labor for hours. He was healthy, weighing in at 8 pounds, but I lost so much blood, I passed out and required blood transfusions. I had spinal headaches from the saddle block and many stitches. My son went home a week before I did. No family could come to support or help us. I endured intense pain that I would not wish on anyone, but beautiful life and much joy came from that suffering that started as a tiny seed.

Once I was well enough to travel after having my son, my husband and I drove to Kentucky. It was winter and close to the time of Christmas and Hanukkah. As we drove, we noticed lights and a huge nativity scene with live animals. We got out of the car to stretch our legs and listen to those gathered under a makeshift stable sing *Silent Night*. The song ended, and many in costumes, including shepherds and the Magi, greeted us. I held my newborn close to my heart and walked over to a lady dressed as Mary (Miriam) who was standing by the manger. I made small talk with the woman and started to walk back to the car. Suddenly, Mary (Miriam) said, "We do not have a baby for the manger, and we are waiting for a member of our congregation to bring a baby doll to place in there, would you want to lay your son in the manger for the next part of our singing? He can play the part of Jesus (Yeshua) in our production, and we even have swaddling clothes." This moment is one I will never forget. My son, who came early, was right on time--all the pain and sorrow from being pregnant at 17 was being bathed in the Father's light.

I had been 3 months pregnant on my wedding day. The pain and shame I felt from my Christian parents were more than I could bear. I had not kept the commandments they had raised me to keep. After the spinal headaches, the medications prescribed to me made it hard to function, let alone with no instructions care for a baby. I was frightened and sure I would make many mistakes with this little one, and I did. I was a baby myself. As we had traveled in the car with our son, I wondered if my parents would accept him and forgive me and healing would take place during our visit. I was praying silent prayers as we drove upon that nativity scene. The Father let me know that even if my family rejected my son, and were still ashamed of me, He was not. The Father was wrapping my newborn in swaddling clothes.

> And she gave birth to her firstborn son and wrapped him in swaddling clothes and laid him in a manger, because there was no place for them in the inn. And in the same region there were shepherds out in the field, keeping watch over their flock by night.
>
> –Luke 2:7-8, ESV

What are swaddling clothes? The prophet Micah reveals the true place of Yeshua's birth: "And you, O tower of the flock, hill of the daughter of Zion, to you shall it come, the former dominion shall come, kingship for the daughter of Jerusalem" (Micah 4:8, ESV). Tradition teaches that there was no room in the inn for Joseph and Mary. Most nativity scenes depict a stable and a feeding trough. The fields of Eder were only steps away from Bethlehem. The tower of the flock was where sacrificial lambs were raised and cared for. Elite shepherds from the tribe of Levi would have cared for these lambs to ensure they remained without spot or blemish like our Messiah. The sheep were pampered and wrapped in fine linen, more than likely the priestly garments until they were sacrificed. [1]

Babies in the womb are wrapped in their own type of swaddling clothing. They are protected and fed through a cord. The placenta delivers oxygen to the baby even though the baby is bathed in liquid. Interestingly, a placenta looks like a tree of life. Its shape and etched branches sprout forth from the cord like a tree whose roots are deeply planted. Our Heavenly Father's fingerprints are all over His creation. The Book of Proverbs expresses that the Father's commandments are said to bring wisdom, which is compared to a tree. When we keep the Father's

---

[1] https://www.chaimbentorah.com/2020/12/hebrew-word-study-tower-of-the-flock-2/

teachings and instructions, we gain wisdom that is more precious than gold. "She [wisdom] is a tree of life to those who take hold of her, and happy are those who hold on to her" (Proverbs 3:18, NASB). We, too, are compared to trees, and our root system is vital. Our sap and our offspring need to know that there is a Creator, and He has given us instructions that, when obeyed, bring life and joy. Derek Markham's recent blog titled *Trees Talk to Each Other and Recognize Their Offspring* is quite eye-opening.

> Now, we know we all favor our own children, and I wondered, could Douglas fir recognize its own kin, like mama grizzly and her cub? So we set about an experiment, and we grew mother trees with kin and stranger's seedlings. And it turns out they do recognize their kin. Mother trees colonize their kin with bigger mycorrhizal networks. They send them more carbon below ground. They even reduce their root competition to make elbow room for their kids. When mother trees are injured or dying, they also send messages of wisdom on to the next generation of seedlings. So we've used isotope tracing to trace carbon moving from an injured mother tree down her trunk into the mycorrhizal network and into her neighboring seedlings, not only carbon but also defense signals. And these two compounds have increased the

resistance of those seedlings to future stresses. So trees talk. ²

– Simard

Similar to tree roots, our voices are always speaking and sending out messages to our children, family members, our friends, and even our enemies. Our trees feed others. Not only is wisdom compared to a tree of life, but the Holy Spirit is described using feminine nouns. This is not to say the Holy Spirit is a woman. God is neither a man nor a woman, yet the Father has attributes of both genders. Can you hear the mothering comforter speaking through the Lord's Son? "How often I have longed to gather your children together, as a hen gathers her chicks under her wings, but you were unwilling!" (Matthew 23:37). The Father describes Israel in the book of Isaiah with a mother's heart: "Thus says the LORD who made you {Israel}, who formed you from the womb and will help you:" (Isaiah:44:2, ESV). The Lord is more compassionate and nurturing than some mothers: "But Zion said, "The LORD has forsaken me; my Lord has forgotten me." "Can a woman forget her nursing child, that she should have no compassion on the son of her womb? Even these may forget, yet I will not forget you" (Isaiah 49:14-15, ESV). Continuing in Isaiah, the Father comforts like a mother: "As one whom his mother comforts, so I will comfort you;" (Isaiah 66:13,

---

² http://www.rapidshift.net/trees-talk-to-each-other-and-recognize-their-offspring/

ESV). Alejandro Jodorowsky, a Chilean filmmaker, and essayist wrote, "No matter how much of an affinity you have for your maternal grandmother or the childhood memories you have of her, you are attached to her through your genes." Not only that, but the emotional experiences of the maternal grandmother can also be passed on to her daughter and granddaughter. Virtuous mothers and righteous fathers are like these trees that send wisdom to the next generation.

The tree of life is a precious gift. Life is worth living. Life continues even when we pass on. The cliché that we have been given a gift each day holds much truth. What will we do with this wondrous day God has given us filled with joy and sorrow? Tree's inhale and exhale. The rocks praise Adonai-- the trees clap their hands and shout with joy. They feed their young, and we are told to feed His lambs. "Simon, son of John, do you love Me more than these?" He said to Him, "Yes, Lord; You know that I love You." He said to him, "Tend (feed) My lambs" (John 21:15, NASB).

Peter had sorrow. He had denied the Messiah. He was close to Yeshua and even walked on water, but now he is filled with sorrow. Yeshua is calling him by name. He is a personal savior. Each time the Master asked Peter if he loved him, the sorrow intensified. Peter would never forget that moment filled with sorrow and joy. He had sorrow that he had denied Yeshua three times. He had joy that the Holy One still found him worthy to feed His lambs.

The Father knows when your weeping of the night is completed and when the morning dove coos with everlasting hope. Life is the tree we eat from. Life is the words we must speak. Life is what fills an empty womb and flees an empty tomb. Today, if you feel lifeless, empty, ashamed, or filled with regret, grab hold of the Master's Hand and wait for Him. Our Father is faithful. He will give you life and life more abundantly. The same God who saw Peter, saw me, a broken, fragile mother traveling home filled with sorrow and joy. The Father took my ashes years ago and He gave me beauty. He wrapped my son in His blankets of light. He wants to do the same for you.

PART 1

Review

1. Can you name a time when the Father gave you beauty in exchange for your ashes?

2. How can we heal from past mistakes and regrets?

3. Sarah laughs and has great joy because she waited a long time for the promise. What does this teach us about His timing and seasons?

4. Multiple things had to align in order for me and my son to end up at the nativity scene at that moment, even an early birth. Can you name a time when the Father ordered your steps to bring healing?

5. The Father compares His instructions and commandments to a tree of life when kept. Knowing this, how does this change your perspective on the fruit of the Spirit Paul mentions in Galatians? "But the fruit of the Spirit is love, joy, peace, patience, kindness, goodness, faithfulness, gentleness, self-control. . ." (Galatians 5:22-23, ESV).

PART 2

Love thyself

The most terrible poverty is loneliness and the feeling of being unloved.

—Mother Teresa

One of the most challenging commandments for some of us to practice is the ability to love ourselves. Yeshua said, "You shall love your neighbor as yourself" (Mark 12:31, NASB). But what measure of love can we give to a broken world if we do not fall in love with who we are and who He created us to be? Find a mirror; run and look at yourself with His eyes. His heavenly hands formed you. Masterful fingertips were shaping eyes and painting them with hues unique to only you. Your mind and thoughts and gifts are here to serve a purpose. His hands wrapped you in light and fed you in the womb. Look at your reflection and say aloud, "I am awesomely and wonderfully made; Wonderful are Your works, And my soul knows it very well" (Psalm 139:14, NASB). You may have never noticed how amazing you are. Yes, I am talking to you. Each freckle, scar, mole, and wrinkle are all signs of life. Like trees, we shed leaves, change hair colors, and stretch our branches towards the heavens. Living things grow. Dead things do not. Sometimes we lose our identity along the way or perhaps never found it to begin with. With the busyness of life, work, tasks to complete, motherhood, and fatherhood, we often need silence and the therapy of being alone with our authentic selves. Sometimes we need to ask ourselves out on a date.

When I first was divorced years ago, I was not used to the sound of silence. I left home at 17, married a military man, and started having babies. I was now 30 and had never experienced silence. Not even the car rides home from work because I either had the radio on or was on my phone or both. The first weekend my ex came to pick up my children, I thought the walls would collapse and the silence would deafen me. I started taking a book and the crossword puzzle from the newspaper to the local Waffle House. I would sit at the bar top counter and drink coffee, order a pecan waffle, and strike up a conversation with usually the person who sat next to me. After I tackled this type of eating alone in public, I ventured to bookstores or coffee houses, but I never tackled my fear of silence and loneliness.

During the pandemic, many of us experienced extreme loneliness. There have been some who died alone with no human touch. But there has always been a pandemic of feeling alone and that no one cares. Almost every one of us has experienced a dark period in our lives. We can be in a room full of people celebrating and feel as dry and parched as a camel trekking through the desert. We can spend hours on websites interacting, commenting, growing our friend lists on social media or hours counting our "likes" and page views, getting the degree, the dream job, a new marriage, and, amidst the applause and approval, be incredibly lonely or feel dead inside. There is a longing to fill an emptiness inside each of our souls that is louder than any sound we will ever hear, and without Yeshua, the Messiah, our souls can be as empty as the tomb on resurrection morning.

How can we reach a point where we understand and feel this loneliness for what it is? Can we sit up straight and look loneliness in the eye with all her shades of barrenness, nakedness, and emptiness and ask, Loneliness, who am I? The Creator of all knows. What is my soul longing for? Why am I here? Alone? What am I created to do? Father, why can't I see my own beauty and strength? Why do I not cherish my very breath—this precious life you have given me? Why haven't you sent me a mate? Or why doesn't my spouse know how empty and unfulfilled I feel?

What if we were to drink in loneliness and depression like a hot herbal tea with honey allowing it to do its complete work without calling someone on our cell phones, leaving the house, or getting on social media to drown out the sound of silence? Silence is loud. Silence rushes into a room and, at times, suffocates us. The walls lean inward and asks us where our true friends are? Family? Mate? Anyone? The echoes of loneliness ricochet off our hearts. In this empty place, this place of silence and waiting, instead of chasing noise or trying to better ourselves, we quiet our soul like a weaned child. We begin to like ourselves. We start to dab cream and massage the bags that sit under our eyes. We send the children to spend time with their fathers, aunts, grandmothers, or another level of the house. Instead of a quick shower, we wrap our hair up and soak in a salt bath. We recognize that we deserve to light a candle for our soul and gently sit it on the edge of the tub. We speak to ourselves differently. Instead of saying things like, I'm getting so old, ugly, fat, skinny, useless, stupid, and unworthy, we begin to wash our skin and love it. We tell ourselves we are a pot on His kiln spinning into perfection. From glory to glory. And when that voice filled with dark words erupts, we say, "shhh, hush now." "Surely I have composed and quieted my soul; Like a weaned child rests against his mother, My soul is like a weaned child within me" (Psalm 131:2, NASB).

In silence, we begin to wrap our souls in garments of grace and give Him our shame, our gaping places, or we soak in the pain — the fellowship of His suffering. Yeshua stands before us, holding out a cup. He asks us the same question He asked His disciples, "Can you drink from the cup that I drink?" We raise the cup to our parched lips and take in the reality of carrying a cross and dying to ourselves. We allow His surgical knife to cut away our rotten flesh. And unexpectedly, one day, without any warning, we are mesmerized by a sunrise, a tree in bloom, birds singing, and tiny insects we never noticed in such intricate details. We plunge our fingers in the dirt and plant things that grow, blossom, and produce fruit. We stop and look at our children with fresh eyes. We acquire eyes that disregard every wrinkle on our mother's face and see her smile. We watch our aging father stooped over, shuffling to the kitchen to put the kettle on, and it is the most beautiful thing we have ever seen. Life is full of wonder and aging. Like the seasons that change, winter will come to us all with its frosty winds and majestic white landscapes covered in snow, pure white snow, and grey hair from a head that has experienced a long life and acquired wisdom.

In the silence, if we will allow it, there is a strange remedy at work—a slowing down. We no longer feel the need to have attention placed on us or to give unneeded attention to those distractions that come. We stop craving the approval of our colleagues, friends, or family. We have no titles as they have dropped off or burned off. We are excited about the rose bushes, a bird singing, and the threading of a sewing machine. Others can no longer define our worth by their nods, grimaces, or looks of disapproval. We no longer seek refreshing water from social media, shopping malls, wine bottles, prescription drugs but, instead, find the refreshing water.

> Everyone who drinks of this water will thirst again, but whoever drinks of the water that I will give him shall never

thirst; but the water that I will give him will become in him a well of water springing up to eternal life. The woman said to Him, "Sir, give me this water, so I will not be thirsty nor come all the way here to draw.

–John 4:13-15, NASB

The Master has spiritual water, and like trees or plants, humans cannot bear good fruit without cultivating the soil. We need fertilizer, water, and sunlight, but we all start as a seed.

> For a seed to achieve its greatest expression, it must come completely undone. The shell cracks, its insides come out and everything changes. To someone who doesn't understand growth, it would look like complete destruction.
>
> –Cynthia Ocelli

You, my friend, are changing. And the seed buried under the dark winter nights will come forth and bloom with fragrant flowers and fruit—precious fruit. "Ho! Everyone who thirsts, come to the waters; And you who have no money come, buy and eat. Come, buy wine and milk Without money and without cost" (Isaiah 55:1, NASB).

PART 2
Review

1. Do you love yourself more than you did last year? How do you know?

2. How does having a negative critical view of ourselves and who He created us to be, stifle our gifts and callings?

3. If we are to love our neighbor as ourselves, on a scale of 1 to 10, how are you doing in this area? What do you love about yourself?

4. What creative, therapeutic things do you do to quiet your soul?

5. How has His Creation helped you see the beauty of life?

Jumping for Joy In the Midst of Sorrow

PART 3

The tornado of 1974

In 1974 I was 8 years young. Certain things never leave our minds. April 3 is one of those memories tucked inside my mind. I remember this day and night well. We had the radio on. The news reporter said the tornado was headed our way. It would cover 13 states before dissipating. We had no basement, and my parents did not seem to be the least bit worried. This was good and bad for the 8-year-old me. At one point, my dad went outside in the gust to survey the skies and get a look at this dark roaring wind. I do remember my parents praying and asking God to protect our loved ones and us. Right before the tornado hit, it got deadly quiet. The air had a strange feel to it. It was a silence that was deafening. No cricket chirped, no bird sang, no tree limb moved. The Super Outbreak of April 3, 1974, stands alone as the most widespread and raging tornado outbreak in recorded history. Meteorologist Jeremy Kappell gives staggering facts recorded from that fearful day.

In total, the event spawned a staggering 148 confirmed tornadoes that impacted 13 states across the Eastern US from New York and Michigan all the way down into parts of Alabama and Mississippi. One twister even crossed into Windsor, Canada. It wasn't just the sheer number of tornadoes that made this outbreak stand out as one of a kind. It was the strength and longevity of these storms. In total, 64 storms reached at least F-3 in intensity with 23 F-4's, and unbelievably, six achieved F-5 statuses. To put this into perspective, the United States, on average, sees less than one F-5--EF-5 each year, and on this day, there were SIX of them!

–April 3-4, 1974 - The Super Outbreak, WDRB News

F5 tornadoes are estimated to have had maximum winds between 261 mph and 318 mph. These dark, whirling winds tear through everything they contact. They toss up cars, school buses, cows, dogs, and anything that gets in their way. They flatten houses, giving them the appearance of toothpicks. These tornados come with a high-pitched eerie sound that you never forget. Thankfully, we were not hit by its destruction, but many close to us in the vicinity were.

The day after the horrific devastation our family got inside our station wagon and drove through areas not blocked off to survey the aftermath. I will never forget driving through rural areas and seeing houses that later made the newspapers. The owners had doors painted red, some had red crosses, others had the sign on the doorpost featuring the Exodus and God's word for the Israelites.

> The blood shall be a sign for you, on the houses where you are. And when I see the blood, I will pass over you, and no plague will befall you to destroy you, when I strike the land of Egypt. "This day shall be for you a memorial day, and you shall keep it as a feast to the LORD; throughout your generations, as a statute forever, you shall keep it as a feast.
>
> —Exodus 12:13-14, ESV

April 3-4, 1974 was a significant date on the Jewish calendar. It was *Ta'anit Bechorot*, Fast of the First Born, for the Hebrew Year 5734. The Fast of the Firstborn is a unique fast day in Judaism which usually falls on the day before Passover.

> It is an ancient and widespread custom for the firstborn to fast on the day before Passover. This commemorates the miracle which spared the firstborn Jewish sons from the plague which struck down the firstborn sons of the Egyptians.
>
> —By Eliyahu Kitov

The day before April 3, 1974, was just another day for many. We never know when destruction will blow through our lives or our families. Like 911, September 11, 2001, is now a memory America will never forget. Each day brings its own trouble, even days that never reach the scale of an F-5. Yeshua reminds us not to worry about tomorrow. "Therefore do not worry about tomorrow, for tomorrow will worry about itself. Today has enough trouble of its own" (Matthew 6:34, BSB). Worrying can take over small situations and create larger ones. We can worry for years about various circumstances, our minds imagining the worst outcomes that never materialize. There are times when we, too, feel like a whirlwind of destruction has blown through our lives or families. Many times what's left of the broken pieces looks unrepairable. We cannot seem to face the damage, or we try to deny any damage has occurred. Sometimes our hearts feel too much. Other times they are numb and calloused. Pain comes in shades of blood-red anger, purple bruises, and intense anguish. It is a sorrowful cumbersome heaviness that often weighs us down. Many times we are carrying hidden pain that no one can see. Often even our laughter comes from a dry well and cackles in the air. There is pain which seeps through pores and reminds us of Yeshua sweating drops of blood and begging for prayer. During the storms of our lives, we try and awaken our friends in the night for help, but sadly their intentions fall by the wayside as they slumber through our most difficult seasons, oblivious to our burdens.

During the day, we place on smiles for our children, spouses, aging parents while walking around bleeding internally. The sorrow erupts as we run the bathwater, sort the laundry, make out the bills, or wipe the snotty nose of a three-year-old.

Sometimes we feel as if Niagara Falls will erupt or the famous geyser Old Faithful from the volcanic activity beneath the surface. We keep pushing all the junk down, but we know it's just a matter of time before we cannot contain our emotions.

Sometimes this sorrow and pain are expressed among close friends, but we only discuss the outer edge of the pie and never get to the center. The cherries are too sour, and the tartness might run off our guest. We speak of the burnt crust and the outer edge of our grief while adding a scoop of ice cream to soothe the truth. Like Hoover Dam, we guard the flood gates. We medicate with antidepressants for fear we might shock those closest to us, and they, in return, would lose the idea they have of our perfect family. We have become accustomed to the words they speak to us over conversations where compliments run thick like molasses. And yet, underneath the smiles and social chatter, we are one step away from collapsing on the floor. The routines that lack vulnerability stifle us. Like an aged book on a shelf, our stories stand covered in cobwebs, yellowed pages, outdated and dogeared.

At the beginning of the Bible, we read about pain, disobedience, nakedness, and murder, all before the 5th chapter of Genesis. Pain continues throughout the Book in multiple layers of conflicts, trauma, betrayal, heartache, and suffering. By the 7th chapter of the Bible, the Creator of all life is so grieved that He has made man that He is going to destroy them all except eight souls. The God who fashioned a woman and man and placed them in the garden of paradise in Genesis 2 speaks in Genesis 6 the most gut-wrenching words in the whole Book.

> Then the LORD saw that the wickedness of man was great upon the earth and that every inclination of the thoughts of his heart was altogether evil all the time. And the LORD regretted that He had made man on the earth, and He was grieved in His heart. So the LORD said, "I will blot out man, whom I have created, from the face of the earth—every man and beast and crawling creature and bird of the air—for I am grieved that I have made them."
>
> –Genesis 6:5-7, BSB

The Father of Glory feels. He has emotions. He suffers. He sees. He weeps. He looked down and saw the violence, child abuse, sex trafficking, and man's beastly nature full-blown and boiling over, and He could not look upon it anymore. Sorrow often comes as a result of our sins and the sins of those around us. The Creator of the heavens and the earth had regrets. He regretted He made man.

Our Father promised never to flood the earth again. He placed a rainbow in the sky. The day after the destructive tornados on April 3rd and 4th of 1974, something memorable happened; bright rainbows and double rainbows appeared in the skies over many states. I remember that moment too. Again, the whole family was outside, looking up at the glorious colors.

Instead of darkness and destruction, there was an arch of colors symbolizing our Father's mercy. My family held no iPhone to capture its beauty. There were no distractions. We were simply awestruck by the splendor and symbol of this promised bow.

Multiple stories involving pots of gold at the end of rainbows can be found. One of the most famous tales involved a poor farmer and his wife in Ireland. The husband and wife pulled their last carrot out of their garden, surprised to find a leprechaun dangling from the roots. Once the leprechaun realized he was captured, he promised one wish in exchange for his freedom. The husband and wife could not decide on just a solitary wish. Like many of us, their minds began dreaming of everything from a new house, a boat, new tools, fine diamonds, fame, and more. They continued dreaming until the leprechaun interrupted them because he was so appalled by their greed. The leprechaun told the couple they could have all they wished for if they found his pot of gold hidden at the end of the rainbow. The leprechaun left them to chase rainbows and pots of gold.

We can chase rainbows and get so caught up in the big picture frame. We miss the simplicity of life and the moments that make up our days. Sometimes morning comes, and we are still mourning the destruction of a past life. We can't shake the tornado that came through years ago. We've lost the tools or the willpower to salvage what is still good and part with the things that no longer can be repaired. After the destruction of 1974, many buildings had to be rebuilt. Sometimes we attempt this rebuilding with broken relationships, but the other parties offer us no rainbow, no mercy, no listening ear. Perhaps your tornado or storm destroyed a marriage, removed a child, or brought a scary diagnosis? How can we find an ounce of joy in such pain? Everyone has a story, a journey, an experience that has wrecked them and caused them to wonder why they are still here—still breathing. And sometimes, the measure and weight of the storms we've survived cause us to hold other broken souls with all the love we needed on the darkest night of our journeys. Sometimes joy comes from doing just that.

If you've experienced great sorrow and suffering and can't seem to pull the sheet back or draw the curtains, just know God sees you. The Bible is full of examples of sorrowful souls waiting for redemption. Naomi, the Lord, watched you bury your sons and husband and knows the weight of your sorrow. He sees you, Ruth. He sees your darkened skin and works in the fields to feed Naomi. He has a plan for you both that will bring you great joy. He sees you, Hannah. He hears your prayers and counts your tears. He sees you, Sarah, and your womb that is dried up. He knows exactly when you will laugh and name your son Isaac a name that means laughter. He sees you, David, running from your father-n-law. He hears your psalms and declares you are a man after His heart, and he will crown you king over all Israel at the exact moment you are fully equipped. And your psalms will be read and sung all over the world and meditated upon. He sees you, Joseph. He sees you in the pit, wrongly accused, and thrown in prison. He has given you every gift needed, the wisdom, knowledge, and understanding to save a people. He sees you, Esther, and he knows that you will be faithful and fearless to save your people and declare a fast and humbly bow before a king to revoke the charges against your people. The God who created the heavens and earth is not a God far away or unreachable. He is a Father close by. He is a God of restoration and promises.

We, too, have the promised comforter, and in the face of grief and emptiness, the wind blows, the Father bows His head to hear us. He gathers us under His Wings of protection like a storm shelter, and He speaks to the harsh storms; peace be still, and we breathe in and release it all to the wind. Stand tall, beautiful Son flowers for you will reap a harvest if you faint not.

PART 3

Review

1. Have you ever experienced destruction that left you paralyzed to the point you did not know how to move forward or pick up the pieces of your life?

2. What emotions do you feel when reading Genesis 6, when the Creator of all was grieved He made man?

3. Do you still find wonder when you see the rainbow? What memories does it evoke from your childhood?

4. In the story of the farmer and his wife, the leprechaun was grieved over the greed of their hearts. How do we store up treasures in heaven while on earth?

5. Do you find it hard to enjoy the moments that make up your life, even in the mundane day to day routines?

SECTION # 2

Mirrors of Truth

The next three devotionals focus on self-awareness, and the joy and sorrow of seeing our strengths and weaknesses.

> *For anyone who hears the word but does not carry it out is like a man who looks at his face in a mirror, and after observing himself goes away and immediately forgets what he looks like.*
>
> *–James 1:23-24, BSB*

Jumping for Joy In the Midst of Sorrow

PART 1

Joyful Outcast

Sometimes joy arrives in the strangest of circumstances. It often comes from those deemed outcasts. It takes a conversation with a homeless veteran to remind us that we have heat blowing through vents in our homes. It takes our car breaking down for us to realize the joy of transportation. Gratitude often brings joy. At other times, it takes a person in a room that we do not want to be labeled as being seen with, like the woman with the alabaster box, to teach us about the oil of gladness for the spirit of mourning. The Pharisees rebuke Yeshua. "If this man (Yeshua) were a prophet He would know who and what sort of person this woman is who is touching Him, that she is a sinner" (Luke 7:39, NASB). All the eyes in the room were on one woman who they deemed unworthy. They were so blind they could not see that the greatest prophet who ever lived was right there in their midst.

One night, years ago, before a conference with a pastor, a small group of those of us in ministry had gathered outside the sanctuary. We were all talking on couches when several others came and sat with us. Some who came for healing and prayers each week, had issues with mental health, trauma, and abuse. One was convinced he was the anti-Christ. Many, like him, were coming to these meetings for prayer, healing, and love. One night, a woman, who made the ministry team uncomfortable due to her beady eyes, strange sense of humor, and continuous mirth at all the wrong moments, sat across the way from me. We will call her Brenda. Brenda began to talk, tease, and chatter to the persons next to her. Brenda rode a public transit bus there and had some form of disability.

I glanced at her backpack on wheels with its Jesus stickers and hearts and pondered her idiosyncrasies. She had never married or had children. One by one, I watched people scurry away from her. Suddenly, they were in need of using the restroom or began to gather into another area by the coffee machine, but Abba whispered to me at that moment—"see her." "Tekoa, do you want to be with the elite? Love my sheep with all the love and even more than you have for these you are looking up to—these who are impressed by Biblical knowledge—these who have asked you to speak on Thursday night-- because Tekoa, I am not impressed." Heart conditions.

I, out of everyone there, should have understood. I was the child who was dragged down the hallway by my sister and the principal in the first year of my schooling--crying, gagging, and kicking as I went. I was the last one picked for sporting events in

P.E. I was the shy pigeon-toed girl who sat at lunch in elementary school alone at times. Children were holding their noses at my smelly paper sack lunch with hard-boiled eggs that stank. Young children, and later teenagers, often were making fun of me. I learned to throw my food away on the way to elementary school. I was ganged in Middle school by a group of girls who beat my head into an aluminum fence so severely that I could not wash my hair for a week. I learned to disappear in a room. Now I was watching adults do what was done to me. They were treating her as if she were a ghost, invisible, and without worth.

I walked over and sat next to this woman created by my Father and began to make small talk. I eased into the chair and complimented Brenda's colorful stickers adorning her travel case. I began to ask her things and smile. I looked deeper into her tiny eyes and imagined His eyes shining back at me. I tried to ignore that it was summer, and she was wearing thick tights the color of a 1990s hunter-green kitchen countertop, or that her paisley mauve dress looked dated from 1940, or how she cracked 3rd-grade jokes, laughing hysterically. And then I began to ask Brenda about her life—dreams—aspirations. Mostly what I remember is this woman in her 40s started crying buckets of tears. She began telling me about her pain. She had lost her father at an early age. As she opened her heart and began to share more, I realized she had experienced much heartache and anguish in her life. And underneath the strange mirth used to mask fears and awkward spaces was a soul that needed to be loved. What an honor it is to listen and love the broken, the strange, the misfits, the sick, the elderly and the ones no one sees or pretends not to see. There is joy in this type of ministry if we are obedient to the call. We help bear burdens, for we are told to do just that. "Bear one another's burdens, and thereby fulfill the law of Christ" (Galatians 6:2, NASB).

Friends, this is what the Body of Messiah needs. And at that moment, as I was sitting on the couch next to Brenda, I recognized that she could have been my mother, misunderstood at a Tupperware party attired in pink lipstick and eyeliner, in a room full of religious spirits. If we think it does not exist in our newfound Torah fellowship, our smiling Joel stadium, our small rural congregation, our shul, our synagogue, we might need to find a mirror. The lady with the piercing blue eyes and the hunter green stockings unfolded the sad details of her life articulately. Oh, how much childlike love she had for Abba. I felt smaller than small. I tried to imagine all the ones He created and shaped on His potter's wheel that we ignore—angels unaware.

Sometimes we hurt--we judge--or we think we know what could come forth from another's heart. These are the ones we have prayed will stop talking, stop speaking, stop praying, and fade into the background of our lives. The lepers are crying out. Can you hear them? They scream, "Son of David have mercy on me!" while the crowd tries to shut their mouths. "Have mercy," they roar as we hurry to the other side of the street or the room, or worse, we pretend we do not hear them or see them at all.

> Jesus replied and said, "A man was going down from Jerusalem to Jericho, and he encountered robbers, and they stripped him and beat him, and went away leaving him half dead. And by coincidence a priest was going down on that road, and when he saw him, he passed by on the other side. Likewise a Levite also, when he came to the place and saw him, passed by on the other side. But a Samaritan who was on a journey came upon him; and when he saw him, he felt compassion, and came to him and bandaged up his wounds, pouring oil and wine on them; and he put him on his own animal, and brought him to an inn and took care of him."
>
> –Luke 10:30-34, NASB

Another story from Matthew 15, reminds me of the outcast and broken. There was a Canaanite woman whose daughter was vexed with demons, and she was in great need, but what did Yeshua's chosen men say at that time?

> Leaving that place, Jesus withdrew to the district of Tyre and Sidon. And a Canaanite woman from that region came to Him, crying out, "Lord, Son of David, have mercy on me! My daughter is miserably possessed by a demon." But Jesus did not answer a word. So His disciples came

and urged Him, "Send her away, for she keeps crying out after us."

–Matthew 15:21-23, NASB

She keeps laughing too loudly. She has dirty laundry. She is embarrassing. She is a Canaanite. I'm too tired. The healthy, chosen disciples, who one day would ponder which side--the right or the left--they could sit in His kingdom, had not yet acquired compassion or empathy for a Canaanite woman with a daughter who was demon-possessed. It was not their problem. Who cares if her daughter screams all night—hisses—put holes in the walls—wears green stockings--not our problem? "Send her away," we cry! Can you hear my voice echoing from amongst Yeshua's disciples? Can you hear yours? We, like them, wait to do what is right—what we know is right. We must picture them as someone's son, someone's daughter, mother, father, sister, brother, and possibly what we do for others will be poured back out on those we love. Those we are praying for daily.

Sometimes people with titles who are well known get better treatment, and we make sure to respond to them quickly. Sometimes cliques happen, and the people in them do not even know that they have formed a group of elites—big dogs. We can walk in a room and feel loved, cherished, and wanted, or we can walk in a room and feel like a square peg among a group of circles. We can walk in a room with new eyesight and compassion, but we usually do not acquire this change without being crushed, rejected, slandered, and unheard. We might not receive what the Father has for our hands to do If we are turning away instead of turning towards those in need. The place lacking an ounce of joy comes from our self-seeking, our arrogance, our knowledge without humility that lacks power. The joy of the Lord Adonai is our strength. Great joy comes from anointing the sick, listening to the outcast, and having empathy for those who suffer in silence. There is nothing more powerful than being chosen to pour oil on the Body of Messiah when we play a part in a person's freedom, healing, and growth by making disciples and by feeding His sheep.

The leaders who pointed at the woman with the alabaster box while she anointed Yeshua proclaimed He was not a prophet, for if Yeshua were, He would see just what kind of woman she was. Friends, may we bow lowly at His Feet regardless of what those in the room are saying. May we minister to a broken world and His broken Body for this brings true joy. A King is coming, so we must work while we still have light. There is so much joy in caring for others and loving our neighbors as ourselves.

PART 1

Review

1. Why does joy seem to erupt when we minister to others?

2. Have you ever felt unloved in a room full of people who proclaim His Name?

3. Why does man look at the outward appearance? Education? Titles? How do these things affect our eyesight?

4. Joy is not in things. Joy cannot be purchased. Name one of your most joyful memories that happened when you least expected it.

5. If you were to define joy, how would you describe it?

PART 2

Suffering Servants

I once was asked by a man in leadership to drive to Bardstown, Kentucky, and pray for a sick woman. She had a tumor that covered half her face, and it came from her eyeball that looked like a cyclops. The first time I saw her and laid hands on her I thought I might throw up--not from her oozing eye but from the feeling of inadequacy to do anything for her. I cried out for Abba to heal her. The appearance of her face was shockingly horrifying. I have no words to describe it. "Have mercy Abba, have mercy," I wept.

One afternoon, as the congregation was having a woman-of-valor type conference with food and fun, I, on the other hand, was headed to pray and clean this woman's home and bathe her. The title of the conference was how to be a servant. Of course, I am talking about a good twelve to fourteen years ago, so I was still relatively immature. I could not do my hidden offerings. I had to announce them. I could not just do good deeds and feel honored that the Messiah had chosen me. I could not store up heavenly treasures because I wanted my reward now. I secretly was pointing fingers at all the women who were having fun, and who was the real servant? Well, I thought it was me, of course! With my chest pumped out and my pride in hand, I judged them--and weren't they healthy? I was too sick to drive to the ailing woman's house. I had to ask my brother to take me. I felt the women were just self-seeking. Mirrors, I needed one badly. I could not see that I had my own eye trouble. I needed to take the plank out of my eye to remove the splinter from my sisters in Christ.

The lessons learned from my travels and ministry have been many. I want to present to you a dilemma: you and I have been selected to host a banquet or a feast among the most prestigious men/women of the day. They are the most affluent. The most wonderful food, drinks, furnishings are being prepared. It is a joyful celebration. The guest list includes sports stars, movie stars, musicians, doctors, authors, philanthropists, rabbis, pastors, and men and women of renown. They know the president, the prophet, the baker, the candlestick maker, and the ones who can move them up a notch. They know the Torah and the hidden secrets of Adonai's Word. They can interpret dreams, speak Hebrew and Greek, teach Torah, and they have large followings. We will get to meet those in leadership afterward and drink up their knowledge. We have our guest list made out. It is exciting. But then the Messiah speaks.

> Now He also went on to say to the one who had invited Him, "Whenever you give a luncheon or a dinner, do not invite your friends, your brothers, your relatives, nor wealthy neighbors, otherwise they may also invite you to a meal in return, and that will be your repayment. But whenever you give a banquet, invite people who are poor, who have disabilities, who are limping, and people who are blind; and you will be blessed, since they do not have the means to repay you; for you will be repaid at the resurrection of the righteous."
>
> –Luke 14:12-14, NASB

This message is one meant for not only our church assemblies but our dining room tables. Yeshua did not mean we could not enjoy family or honorable dinner guests, but we may need to reevaluate our heart condition and guest list at times. Yeshua suggests inviting people with special needs. Curiously, these examples given by Yeshua of different ones to invite to our tables may imply their spiritual condition. The church in Laodicea had many of the disabilities listed in Luke 14. "For you say, I am rich, I have prospered, and I need nothing, not realizing that you are wretched, pitiable, poor, blind, and naked" (Revelation 3:17, ESV).

Righteousness requires not only ministering to people with needs but also abstaining from evil but a constant pursuit of justice and mercy and loving our neighbor as ourselves. One night I decided to venture away and spend time in His Word. I opened my Bible to a story that came to life before my eyes like a motion picture movie screen. Yeshua and His disciples were taking a boat ride to a cemetery where two men were naked, deranged, and cutting themselves. They were out of their minds. Their screams penetrated the darkness with thick anguish. Guttural sounds pierced the peace and blanketed the sky with black. Have you ever seen grown men with abscesses oozing, burn marks, and scabs on their skin, men and women addicted to crack, ice, pain pills, and crystal meth swathed in dark circled raccoon eyes that lack emotion? Men who would rob their grandmother and steal their family's possessions to get just one more fix. The disciples stare in horror at the condition of the men before them--men who live among the dead. No one in the town dares to help them, for chains and fetters cannot keep them bound. Their children have given up on them. One of the elders at the gate said that if someone would kill them and toss them in an unmarked grave, the whole city would feel safer. However, on this night, those deranged souls were going to see One so gentle, so loving, and One with such authority the wind and the waves hushed at His command.

Suddenly, Yeshua shows up with eyes that love the most disturbing outcast with such purity one can only compare it to a lamb, a dove, a river, a well that causes one never to thirst. Yeshua, the Messiah, has a love that evokes great power. When Messiah leaves the graveyard, the two men are clothed and in their right mind. There is fantastic joy! Unspeakable joy. Yeshua tells them to go and minister to their families and make disciples. No one in the town can believe it. Dead men, living among the dead, were now full of light and hope and a joy that summoned the dawn!

> As He was getting into the boat, the man who had been demon-possessed was imploring Him that he might accompany Him. And He did not let him, but He said to him, "Go home to your people and report to them what great things the Lord has done for you, and how He had mercy on you." And he went away and began to proclaim in Decapolis what great things Jesus had done for him; and everyone was amazed.
>
> —Mark 5:18-20, NASB

We, too, have a choice every day to shine our lights. We have an opportunity to make a difference in someone's life who is suffering. We can do it with bitterness, pride, going through the motions, or we can do it in love. The Messiah tells us to feed His sheep. Love His sheep. This requires a death. Yeshua was the Son of man, who took the time to heal the deranged. He also journeyed to see one woman at a well. One woman who did not have the facts right.

> "Woman," Yeshua replied, "believe me, a time is coming when you will worship the Father neither on this mountain nor in Jerusalem. You Samaritans worship

what you do not know; we worship what we do know, for salvation is from the Jews."

–John 4: 21-22, NASB

Sometimes those who do not have all their theology correct have a teachable spirit. Yeshua went on to say that He was looking for a specific type of person who would worship Him in spirit and truth. The Samaritan woman grabbed on to His Words and went and preached the gospel to her whole city. This woman at the well became the first Evangelist. 'Then the woman left her water jar, went back into the town, and said to the people, "Come, see a man who told me everything I ever did. Could this be the Christ?" So they left the town and made their way toward Jesus" (John 4:28-30, BSB).

From the men oppressed by demons to the Samaritan woman at the well, our Master Yeshua found them of great importance. He was indeed the humblest servant to ever walk this earth. May we have a guest list that warrants us a spot in the first resurrection. The apostle Paul said he hoped he was found worthy of making the first resurrection. When we get our focus off ourselves and on others, there is great joy and great testimonies. The things done in secret for the outcast, the widow, the homeless, the orphan, and the sick are the most rewarding ministry there is, and James (Jacob) says that this is true and unadulterated. "Pure and undefiled religion in the sight of our God and Father is this: to visit orphans and widows in their distress, and to keep oneself unstained by the world" (James 1:27, NASB).

Prayer is a hand wiping the brow of the sick. It is hands baking bread, cleaning another's home, listening to the sick's cry, and pouring out our love to those in prison, hungry, thirsty, without husbands or fathers, those who weep and need compassion and healing like the men at the tombs who were screaming and cutting themselves. Those living in a place of death need life. I have never visited a hospital, a nursing home, a homeless shelter, or a place where those in great need lived that I did not receive great joy. The joy of the Lord is our strength.

PART 2

Review

1. In Matthew 28 two men were delivered from demons, clothed and in their right minds. Can you think of a person in your life who changed so radically they were unrecognizable? What about your own journey?

2. Have you ever ministered at a soup kitchen or shelter? Did it change you, and if so, how?

3. How are testimonies and joy connected?

4. Have you ever considered wiping a sick person's brow as a type of prayer, or what about feeding a hungry soul?

5. Have you ever given out of your poverty and received great joy from it?

PART 3

Seeing our True Reflection

I once had a friend who was gifted in writing and singing music. One day she called in tears and was being uprooted from her home. I already had two extra people living with me in a modest ranch with only one bathroom. I felt led to tell her to come and stay until she figured things out. Meanwhile, I had a teenage son who was depressed and a dog who had become way overprotective of me due to my sickness. My beloved Rex had begun to bite just about everyone-- except—well, me and my son.

A few weeks later, with so many in the small quarters, I was continuously juggling my dog from my bedroom to the backyard. Rex, in Houdini fashion, had learned to escape by jumping the fence. I had not acquired such skills yet. A month in and with multiple piles of laundry in front of my washer--I felt spent. I decided to have dinner with a friend one night. I left my dog locked in my bedroom for a short duration. During dinner, my latest house guest called to tell me her daughter was coming for the weekend. Her husband had full custody of her daughter, but she got her on the weekends. It had been weeks since she had seen her. She was excited. She was already sleeping on my couch. Where would her daughter sleep? I couldn't breathe.

I remember praying under my breath for Abba to stop the insanity. I could not handle another person, and I was still quite sick from my neurological issues. I screamed silently inside my head, "Abba send her away! I do not want her here." I arrived home after dinner to find more bags and another guest. I tried to smile and be friendly, but inside I was saying, "Release me, Abba." My modest home was at full capacity. Rex was growling from behind the door, and he was a good 100 pounds. I was so fatigued, and now I had to get the leash and take him outside, making sure he did not weasel his way into the neighbor's yard and bite them or one of my new houseguests.

Within minutes of taking the dog out, my friend's daughter felt sick at her stomach. She wanted to leave. She began to cry. She was around fourteen. I tried to console her. I offered food—a Ginger-ale—Tums. Her father picked her up shortly afterward. I was so relieved and quickly made my way outside for fresh air. A few minutes later, my friend came out on the porch where I sat, and she looked at me teary-eyed and said, "Someone prayed for my daughter to leave. Someone has caused this because they didn't want my daughter here!" This is what must have made her sick, and oh how bad I miss her." Tears and anger rolled swiftly off her cheeks. I will never forget that moment-- along with many other splatters of humiliation that have wedged in my brain.

Another example is from years ago. I was asked to share at an assembly with my husband when we were newly married. I was sharing a testimony—no doctrine—no teaching that anyone could inspect with a microscope, but suddenly I could not think right. I could not speak; I had no words. Fumbling, I held the microphone back to my husband. I felt a scorching in my soul. And just like my friend on the porch that night with her antennas out screaming, "Someone prayed for my daughter to leave!" I felt it. I, too, was reasonably sure I knew who it was that was commanding under their breath for my mouth to be shut--the senior pastor at our assembly. About a week later, this pastor sat on my couch in my living room and told me he cringed when my husband handed me the microphone. He did not feel comfortable with me speaking. He was a straight shooter and blunt. Out of the abundance of his heart, he was saying it. How could I not forgive him? I was no better.

At times, I find blunt people more refreshing than the ones who hide behind layers of perfection and never pull their hearts out and show people the cuts, bruises, insecurities, rejections, and weaknesses they have experienced on this journey called life. They appear perfectly put together. We survey fruit like a cantaloupe or an avocado that we need to check for ripeness, or we walk past a mirror and glance at it and never even notice we have a piece of toilet tissue stuck on our shoes. Most of us have never seen ourselves on television or in real-time. We have watched the freshly groomed, cleaned shaven, makeup intact, well-rehearsed versions of ourselves, but we should grab a camera in the middle of a fight with a spouse or a hot day in traffic with a screaming toddler or eight house guests. Well, go on, let us post that on our YouTube channels. No, we don't capture those moments for others to see usually, and we don't see ourselves as others do. If I had to guess, it's probably one way or the other. We see ourselves a little too good, prideful even, or, perhaps, not good at all. Yes, and even that has pity and pride in it--but then there is another far worse issue, our eyes distort our perception. Objects in the rearview mirror may be closer than they seem.

My mother used to wear lovely maxi dresses, which she hand-stitched using McCall's patterns and added adornments. My mother, Vicky, was beautiful and always looked much younger than her years. A lady who lived in the neighborhood had been watching Vicky leave for church and other engagements in her long floral maxi dresses. She came over and inquired about borrowing one of my mother's gowns for a special occasion. My mother weighed about a hundred and thirty pounds, and the woman who stood before her weighed at least three hundred. She thought she could borrow one of my mom's dresses because she, like us at times, kept passing by the mirror and seeing what she wanted to see, reflecting back at her. self-perception.

There is another story about my mother that I will never forget. One day she was invited to a Tupperware party. The party was hosted by a lady whose husband worked with my dad. My mother and his wife were good friends. They were Pentecostals; we were not. I do not think they wore headscarves or Tzitzits, but they had their own attire. Long hair, long dresses, no makeup, and a strict unspoken rule book. My mother showed up at the party with her thick eyeliner, mascara, bleach blonde hair, and a pair of jeans, and a T-shirt from the 1970s that said, *Jesus Loves You*. The women soon gathered in the kitchen, away from my mom. They whispered. They snickered. They made remarks, and my mother overheard Jezebel, harlot, and sinner.

Finally, my mother stood in front of them as the *Tupperware* presentation was coming to a close, and she said, "If you really think I'm a Jezebel headed for hell, shouldn't you have shown me love and told me about your God—my God—our God? Is not love the greatest gift? Won't the world know we are Christians by our love?" You could have heard a pin drop in the room. It was a Harper Valley P.T. A- moment. If you're not familiar with the Harper Valley P.T.A., pull up the old song on YouTube and listen. My mother, in tears, made her way home. Where is the joy? My mother made an impact on religious spirits that day. And as she walked home feeling rejected, despised, a woman of many sorrows, Yeshua whispered, "You are becoming like me. I too was despised and rejected and a man full of sorrow" (Isaiah 53:3). This is the fellowship of suffering that causes us to become one with the Lamb of God. This is the cross. "You will be hated by everyone because of me, but the one who stands firm to the end will be saved" (Matthew 10:22, NIV).

In both stories concerning my mother, lessons were learned through mirrors being held up. In the last story, my mother held a mirror up so those dealing with a spirit of religion could see themselves better. In the first story, a woman mesmerized by my mothers' dresses and beauty thought she was the same size as my mother even though she was twice her size. Disproportions need balance. Both instances have hidden lessons for us all. How do we see ourselves; how do others see us?

Sometimes we learn the most hidden profound truths from sorrow and rejection. Sometimes a heavenly mirror appears, and we experience deep introspection that forever changes us on the inside. "For the LORD sees not as man sees: man looks on the outward appearance, but the LORD looks on the heart" (I Samuel 16:7, ESV).

PART 3

Review

1. Have you ever wanted to shut someone's mouth? Of course, we all have at some point. Herodias had her daughter dance for King Herod. Afterward, Herod offered her up to half the kingdom. Her mother told her to request John the Baptist's head on a platter. What causes people to want the voice of truth snuffed out?

2. How can we be more compassionate for those in need without becoming a doormat?

3. Why is it often difficult to see our true reflection? How can we uncover our weaknesses and strengths to find balance?

4. Why do we often judge people by their covers, titles, and education?

5. Have you ever been my mother at a party? Have you ever been the others who were judging her based on their religious bias?

SECTION # 3

Disability or Divine Calling

The next three devotionals showcase inspirational people, who in spite of their limitations, are producing much fruit.

I can do all things through Christ who gives me strength.

–Philippians 4:13, BSB

Jumping for Joy In the Midst of Sorrow

PART 1

Harriet

Every great dream begins with a dreamer. Always remember, you have within you the strength, the patience, and the passion to reach for the stars to change the world.

–Harriet Tubman

My husband and I recently watched the movie *Harriet*, which depicted the life of Harriet Tubman. If you have not seen the film, it is a must-watch. After bawling through most of it, tears of joy, I wanted to dig deeper and study the books that had been written about the life of Harriet Tubman. I desired to learn more about this woman who was swifter than eagles, more powerful than most men, and given the title of General in the army.

As we watched the movie, I was reminded that in my 4th and 5th-grade class, we students were given the assignment to dress up as someone of importance and read a report about their lives. The class was given a sheet of paper with a list of men and women. I chose Pocahontas in 4th grade and Harriet Tubman in the 5th. My mother looked at me funny and said, "Bonnie, how are we going to dress you up as Harriet Tubman?" I did not think about her skin color because I was astonished that she freed many people, and those people had given her the nickname Moses, and I knew who Moses was. Harriet was born and died in March. This, too, is interesting, considering Moses's birth and death occurred in the same month during this time.

> Moses, the greatest prophet of Israel, was born and died on the 7th day of Adar. It is characteristic of the righteous of Israel that the day which makes their entrance into this world, is the same calendar date which marks their departure from this world and entry into the next world. This is a manifestation of the principle that the righteous fill their days and their years with their good deeds. Therefore, the years of their lives reach perfect completion before they depart from the world. [3]
>
> –Temple Institute

After the movie, I began to dig into Harriet's life. I learned that Harriet and I had several things in common. Her mother's maiden name was Green. My maiden name is Green. We both were born in March; her day of birth is not known, as many slaves' births were not recorded. We both experienced visions and dreams after having suffered damage to the brain. Although

---
[3] https://www.templeinstitute.org/adar-month-of-joy.htm

I have never snatched a thousand people from slavery, I write books and blogs that I pray bring spiritual freedom to some or comfort those who suffer. I am no Harriet Tubman, but the Father sure used her story to comfort me.

I do not think I have ever been so moved by a woman of her caliber or tenacity. Of course, many women come to mind, Corrie Ten Boom, Rosa Parks, Sofka Skipwith, Mother Teresa, and what of the nameless and faceless women who are snatching women and children from the grips of evil daily. Those who risk their lives in the sex trafficking underground to save any they can-- those who house the pregnant unwed, feed the widows, and care for the sick, giving selflessly.

Several pieces of Harriet's life were not depicted in the movie: Her birth name was Araminta—very close to Arminta," which means "Jerusalem Liberated." (Araminta is a hybrid of two other names - but it is not new. It was invented in the 1600s. It's a mashup of Arabella, meaning "yielding to prayer," and "Aminta" meaning "defender). [4]

Harriet's life was both of these. Minty, her nickname, seems to express a breath of fresh air. In 1820 – Harriet Ross Tubman, born Araminta "Minty" Ross, was born a slave in the plantation of Edward Brodess in Dorchester County, Maryland. Her mother was Harriet "Rit" Green, owned by Mary Pattison Brodess, and her father was Ben Ross, owned by Anthony Thomson. The last

---
[4] https://www.scarymommy.com/baby-names/girl-baby-names/araminta/

name Ross means a steed or horse. She was as swift as a horse in freeing many.

In 1825 – Young Araminta was hired out to other households. Her first outside job was as a nursemaid, where she was violently and frequently beaten when she let the baby cry. Can you picture five-year-old Minty made to stay awake all night in case the master's baby cried and then beaten if it did? Harriet was a baby herself. Sadly, history is filled with evil men and women, brainwashed, ignorant, and unashamed. Harriet was later hired to set muskrat traps. Due to the nature of the job, she fell ill and was sent back to Brodess.

In 1833 – Araminta was severely injured in the head with a heavy metal weight aimed at a runaway slave. (She got in front of it to block the one it was intended for). Bleeding and unconscious, she was returned to her owner's house and laid on the seat of a loom, where she remained without medical care for two days. The injustice of it all is mindboggling. Thirteen-year-old Harriet was bleeding out, and no one to show her an ounce of compassion or mercy. The seat of a loom seemed quite prophetic to me as she wove new garments of freedom for those bound in slavery. Afterward, Harriet began to have premonitions and vivid dreams; she said that God communicated with her. Tubman said the metal weight "broke my skull."

A hole in my head made God's voice more clear.

–Harriet.

In the movie's first scene, Tubman experiences one of her "spells," which often caused her to lose conscious and seemed to give her visions of nearby dangers or events to come. Twenty first-century historians have speculated that Tubman might have had narcolepsy, epilepsy, or both.

When Harriet had visions or premonitions, she appeared to be in an unconscious state. She claimed to be aware of her surroundings but appeared to onlookers asleep. This condition remained with her for the rest of her life. It was then that Harriet began experiencing strange visions and vivid dreams, which she ascribed to forebodings from God. This part of her story had me in tears. I flashed back to my own journey and how two lesions on my brain and an attack back in 2006/2007 had left me too sick to work, finish college, or even walk at one point. On the flip side, I was given night visions, dreams, and began to hear in my spiritual ear with great awe. These spiritual happenings left me often living in a world full of strange experiences many would mock if told about.

Adonai's Voice became so loud indeed that after testing it on multiple occasions, I learned to fear this Voice and yet form intimacy with Him in ways I never had before. One day while extremely sick, I heard, "go check your email." This was before cell phones with email and Facebook at our fingertips. I told the Father I was too sick to get up from the couch where I had made my bed for a year. "I will check it later," I pled. The third time I heard His Voice say, "get up and go down the hall to the office and check your mail!" The Voice was loud, and an urgency to be obedient filled my spirit. I picked up my cane and ran my hand along the walk for balance. Once my feet touched the hallway, my entire ceiling imploded. Inside the walls were electrical wires from a heating system in the walls; the ceiling was plaster. On the couch where I had argued with a Voice who created the universe laid a pile of hard plaster, wires, debris, and smoke rising through the air. I stood in the hallway and gazed up at the rafters; empty A-framed timbers held bits of insulation, and I held myself and leaned into the wall. Abruptly, like Harriet, I became aware of the gift of life and how, when I was well and my body was whole I had taken it for granted. I had been requesting to die because of the pain, the loss, and a host of sorrows, but now suddenly, I wanted to live despite my feeling like death. "No!," I said aloud, "I shall not die, but live, and declare the works of the LORD" (Psalm118:17, NKJ).

As my eyes traveled over the room wrecked with rubbish, I knew that I had just witnessed one of His works. The work of our Heavenly Father was evident, but what if I had not heeded the Voice? I learned a great lesson that day about obedience. My son came home to find the front door barricaded, and he had to climb through the bedroom window, but there was not a scratch on me. Most everyone has had an experience where the Father of Glory warned them or spoke to them in some fashion. Still, after this intense suffering and the two lesions on my brain that the neurologist compared to Multiple Sclerosis, I can only say what Harriet said. The scars on my head made His Voice more clear--louder. This is both beautiful and, at times, gut-wrenching.

The pain and suffering Harriet endured is unimaginable. And yet, we call her Moses, and we cheer inside when we read of her bravery. Harriet prayed for the death of her cruel master, and he died. Tubman flees with two of her brothers, who end up returning due to fear. However, she makes a 100-mile journey to freedom with no ability to read and with her frequent seizures and ailments.

After escaping slavery and heading to Pennsylvania, Harriet went back in 1850 and brought her niece and two children to freedom. Over 11 years, Tubman rescued over 70 slaves from Maryland and assisted 50 or 60 others in making their way to Canada. This is around the time she became known as Moses.

"Tubman offered her services to the Union Army, and in early 1862, she went to South Carolina to provide badly needed nursing care for black soldiers and newly liberated slaves. Working with General David Hunter, Tubman also began spying and scouting missions behind Confederate lines. In June of 1863, she accompanied Colonel James Montgomery in an assault on several plantations along the Combahee River, rescuing more than 700 slaves. Her deed was celebrated in the press, and she became even more famous." [5]

After the war, Harriet married a Civil War veteran. In her later years, she was often speaking about women's suffrage and was awarded a nurse's pension in the 1880s. She established the Harriet Tubman Home for the aged on her property and died there surrounded by family and friends. Harriet died on March 10, 1913. She was buried with military honors at Fort Hill Cemetery in Auburn. God buried Moses. "The LORD buried him in a valley in Moab, opposite the town of Bethpeor, but to this day no one knows the exact place of his burial" (Deuteronomy 34:6, GNT).

I love this woman who took on the spirit of Moses. Like Moses, Harriet's hands were always found helping, building, healing, and snatching those in bondage out of Egypt. May we too use all our power as this female Moses did to bring freedom to those suffering, shackled, and in need of a Savior.

---

[5] https://www.battlefields.org/learn/biographies/harriet-tubman

PART 1

Review

1. Do you believe the Father still speaks to His children by sending dreams and visions, according to Joel 2?

2. What characteristics of Moses did Harriet embody?

3. Why must we be set free first in order to free others?

4. Have you ever argued with the Voice of Adonai? If so, what did you learn?

5. Harriet proclaimed a hole in her head made the Voice of the Father louder. What tragedies in your own life have made His Voice louder for you?

Jumping for Joy In the Midst of Sorrow

PART 2

A Golden Ticket

The winepress, olive press, and long-suffering all produce the anointing. In the dark season, under the frozen earth, a seed is coming undone. This dark hidden place is a blanket for the soul giving us character development. This process, once completed, brings joyful buds and a sweet-smelling fragrance of blossoms opening in spring. Opposite of the season of winter is intense heat in the furnace where gold is purified from dross. Joy and purity come from suffering. This process to become holy is the reversal of what many of us have been taught.

Strike that, now reverse it!'

–Roald Dahl

Roald Dahl, author of *Willy Wonka and the Chocolate Factory*, has many hidden gems in his writings. He says strike out what you have been programmed to believe and reverse it. Grandpa Joe, in the movie *Willy Wonka*, got out of his sickbed when his grandson received a golden ticket, but I have some dear friends right now with ALS, MS, RA, etc. that have not been able to get out of bed for years—cannot feed themselves, bathe themselves, or even wipe themselves. Unless our Messiah Yeshua walks into their rooms and heals them, they will be gathered with their loved ones sooner than later. The Father can and does heal, but He has not healed them yet. No golden ticket, Charlie. I have one friend that has been in a nursing home for over a decade—a decade in bed, but she has ministered to me during some of my darkest hours. She ministers from a bed of suffering, typing text on good days with her pinky fingers as her other ones are like crinkled-up french fries due to rheumatoid arthritis.

Time is a precious thing. Never waste it.

–Roald Dahl

But I ask, which person would waste more time, a person disabled or one with good health? All of us are prone to waste valuable time, but I think you will be amazed at some of the people I will cover in this chapter. Many of them could have consumed their whole lives in pity, anger, doubt, and fear but instead have used their suffering to comfort others. They do not have long healing lines wrapped around buildings. They do not make millions or own jets, but what they have sparkles and shimmers from the inside out.

Where is fancy bred? In the heart or in the road?

–Roald Dahl

One day, I asked the Father some questions--perplexing questions. I was feeling overwhelmed by the many sick people He had sent across my path of late. I longed to help them, pray with them, and encourage them, but mostly their situations had not improved. I frequently talk to the Father but usually do not get a quick response, if any, but on this particular day, He astounded me. While meditating on disease and suffering, I suddenly heard this in my spirit.

"Nick Vujicic wouldn't have the ministry he does encouraging people if he had limbs."

Immediately in a type of vision, there Nick was before me smiling. If you don't know who Nick is, he is one of seven known cases in the world of people born with tetra-amelia syndrome, a rare disorder characterized by the absence of arms and legs. According to his autobiography, his mother refused to see him or hold him when the nurse held him in front of her. Still, she and her husband eventually accepted the condition and understood it as "God's plan for their son." His bio is long, but here is a snippet.

"Since his first speaking engagement at age 19, Nick has traveled around the world, sharing his story with millions, sometimes in stadiums filled to capacity, speaking to a range of diverse groups such as students, teachers, young people, business professionals, and church congregations of all sizes." [6]

---

[6] https://coreagency.com/speakers/nick-vujicic/

A scripture popped into my head: "The Father speaks to Moshe, "Who has made man's mouth? Or who makes him mute or deaf, or seeing or blind? Is it not I, the LORD?" (Exodus 4:11, NASB).

And again, I hear, "Nick Vujicic would not have the ministry he does, encouraging people, if he had limbs." What a profound thought. Go to his website, and you will see Nick's smiling photo of him splashing in his swimming pool. There are ministry photos of him speaking to thousands, and one where he is holding a child born with the same disease. But what if Nick were sitting in a wheelchair looking disparaged and weary? Would we see him the same? Would our emotions change? Of course, they would. Some might argue that if the Father healed Nick and he grew limbs, Nick would have a more prominent ministry, but what has given him a flourishing ministry is his attitude and vigor to make something of this precious life regardless of his physical condition. By the way, two of the seven with tetra-amelia syndrome are sportswriters and journalists.

I believe in healing and multiple ways of being healed, but is everyone healed physically? No, not even one of the most righteous missionaries in the Newer Testament. "Greet Prisca and Aquila, as well as the household of Onesiphorus. Erastus has remained at Corinth, and Trophimus I left sick in Miletus" (II Timothy 4:19-20, BSB). The apostle Paul who was anointed to heal many, left this man sick with, more than likely, malaria. The great prophet Elisha died in his disease. Wouldn't men such as these be eating foods that were grown the Torah way? Wouldn't they have a better grasp of anointing oils and laying hands on the sick? Why would the apostle Paul (Sha'ul) tell Timothy to have a little wine for his stomach if a swing of his suit jacket, a dab of oil, and a "By His stripes you are healed" work wonders? Why would Isaiah apply figs as medicine if he could just lay his hands on King Hezekiah and heal him? "Prepare a poultice of figs." So they brought it and applied it to the boil, and Hezekiah recovered" (II Kings 20:7, BSB).

We are often "Wrong, sir, wrong!"

–Roald Dahl

But let's face it: many people with arms and legs are suffering greater than smiling Nick. He encourages people to enjoy life and be thankful, grateful even, but if given enough kale juice, cut out sugar and carbs, slather him in oils, make him repent for any evil thought, Nick will not grow arms and legs. No, not likely to happen. These things work well for the healthy or for the ones who have taken their health for granted and have become couch potatoes.

I want to present a thought: Could Nick be more whole than you and I? More joyful–more thankful? Could Nick be wasting less time than those of us with limbs? Have you ever visited a nursing home, hospital, or orphanage to minister to someone, and they ended up ministering to you? I think we both know this happens every time. A golden ticket, for sure. A parable describes a man named Lazarus who died and went to Abraham's bosom. He was not wealthy or healthy. He was sick and in need of food. He had sores oozing. However, in the next life, it was the wealthy man who was in torment. "Now there was a rich man, and he habitually dressed in purple and fine linen, joyously living in splendor every day. "And a poor man named Lazarus was laid at his gate, covered with sores, and longing to be fed with the crumbs which were falling from the rich man's table; besides, even the dogs were coming and licking his sores" (Luke 16:19-21, NASB).

If you want to view paradise, simply look around and view it.

–Roald Dahl

The parable concerning Lazarus showcases a sick man begging for compassion and bread. The wealthy man passed by him daily but had no empathy or love to give. I have written about sickness before but possibly not in these shades of grey, and the worse I suffer, the more I have to say about it. This topic is not for everyone, but perhaps my take on it will help a few find joy even in great sorrow—even in great pain. Possibly, those who are healthy will see that the sick may have wisdom that comes from suffering. "Although He (Yeshua) was a Son, He learned obedience from the things which He suffered" (Hebrews 5:8, BLB).

Many quote multiple verses on healing with great faith. They use them over and over for friends who just received heartbreaking diagnoses. However, most of these people boldly shouting, "be made whole in Jesus's name," still wear prescription eyeglasses and see a dentist. They take medications for pain or Tylenol on occasion. Possibly many who claim divine healing took the chemo therapy, had the surgery, etc. for extra coverage. If a person with paraplegia or a person with quadriplegia is brought into the room, will those who are shouting verses and natural cures walk over and yell, "Life and death are in the power of the tongue. Stand up and walk! Yeshua came for you to have an abundant life." Would these be inclined to tell the person with paraplegia to eat some kale and drink some pomegranate juice– live the Torah way? Doubtful.

The Messiah did come to give us life and life more abundantly, and Nick is living a life preaching the Gospel and shining light. Even with Nick's lack of arms and legs in the natural, he is spiritually equipped with Yeshua's arms and feet. Lazarus was directly in front of the rich man, but the rich man never cared. The rich man did not medicate his sores or let him eat at his table. It was not the poor beggar Lazarus who needed to be healed. It was a healthy, wealthy man who needed to be healed of a heart condition. Isaiah 53:5, KJV says, "By His stripes, we are healed." This verse is a popular verse used for the sick. Peter used this verse to point out the truth. "And He Himself bore our sins in His body on the cross, so that we might die to sin and live to righteousness; for by His wounds, you were healed" (I Peter 2:24, NASB). Yes, often the verses used for healing are talking about being healed from sin and about the lost sheep of the House of Israel-- instead of a physical infirmity. Is there a measure used when regarding how powerful our Father is? Is someone with poor eyesight or an earache a better candidate to be healed than, say, Nick, growing arms? Why don't we pray to throw out our bifocals at 40? Why did a man who had vigor and perfect eyesight walk up a hill and die? Because God said, Moses, it is time. Because the Father said, it is time, My Son, Yeshua.

> Then the LORD said to Moses, "Behold, the time for you to die is near; call Joshua, and present yourselves at the tent of meeting, that I may commission him." So Moses and Joshua went and presented themselves at the tent of meeting.
>
> –Deuteronomy 31:14, NASB
>
> Although Moses was one hundred and twenty years old when he died, his eye was not dim, nor his vigor abated.
>
> –Deuteronomy 34:7, NASB
>
> *Bubbles, Bubbles Everywhere, But not a drop to drink.*
>
> –Roald Dahl

Yes, most of us want those suffering to get better–to live happily ever after. We do everything out of love, and we want those in anguish to be made whole, but what if the person in front of us is more whole than we are--more filled with joy? Sometimes things are opposite. *"Strike that, now reverse it!"* Psalm 73 is very descriptive to expound on those who prosper in this life.

> Surely God is good to Israel, To those who are pure in heart! But as for me, my feet came close to stumbling; my steps had almost slipped. For I was envious of the arrogant As I saw the prosperity of the wicked. For there are no pains in their death, And their body is fat. They are not in trouble as other men, Nor are they plagued like mankind. Therefore pride is their necklace; The garment of violence covers them. Their eye bulges from fatness; The imaginations of their heart run riot. They mock and wickedly speak of oppression; They speak from on high. They have set their mouth against the heavens, And their tongue parades through the earth. Therefore his people return to this place, And waters of abundance are drunk by them. They say, "How does God know? And is there knowledge with the Most High? Behold, these are the wicked; And always at ease, they have increased in wealth. Surely in vain, I have kept my heart pure And washed my hands in innocence; For I have been stricken all day long And chastened every morning.
>
> —Psalm 73:1-13, NASB

Do you feel stricken and chastened? Job did, Jeremiah did, and many others. One woman's journey was so full of obstacles, disabilities, and sorrow, but her triumph and tenacity inspire many today. Helen Keller was born with much adversity, but she accomplished more than most people who were born with eyes to see and ears to hear.

> *Anything you want to, do it; want to change the world-- there's nothing to it.*
>
> –Roald Dahl

Another inspiring story is the life of Helen Keller. Helen Adams Keller was born on June 27, 1880 and died on June 1, 1968. She was an American author, political activist, and lecturer. She was the first deaf-blind person to earn a Bachelor of Arts degree. The story of Keller and her teacher, Anne Sullivan, was made famous by Keller's autobiography, *The Story of My Life*, and its adaptations for film and stage, *The Miracle Worker*. What would her life have been like if she were born healthy, had perfect vision, and powerful hearing? Awe, but she did. Helen saw and heard things many do not, thanks be to her mentor, Anne Sullivan. Who are you mentoring right now with greatness inside them, things that need to be birthed for future generations? Helen worked with the American Institute for the Blind for 44 years. Keller teamed up with the Jewish Institute for the Blind. She spoke words with great chutzpa to those who tried to blind society and close their eyes to injustices. Here is one such quote from 1933.

One of the most powerful pieces in the Keller archive is a letter to the Student Body of Germany, written in 1933. The German universities had been burning books that contradicted their evil agenda, including a book that Helen herself had written on socialism and social justice, and hearing of it shortly afterward, Helen's anger and sharp words warned the Nazis.

"History has taught you nothing if you think you can kill ideas.

Do not imagine your barbarities to the Jews are unknown here.

God sleepeth not, and He will visit His Judgment upon you." [7]

Helen, who could neither see the enemy nor hear the raging voice of Hitler with her natural ear, did hear with a heart that took action and with courage. Would Helen Keller be the same bold, compassionate woman without her disabilities? Without her teacher, Sullivan? Perhaps, but doubtful in the measure of tenacity she exuded. How many people with spiritually closed ears and eyes laid hands on her or prayed for her to see while they sat blind and naked without hunger or passion? We can have 20/20 vision and be blind as a bat.

Friends, we must rethink some things. No matter what you are going through today may these two individuals' lives be

---

[7] https://www.oneforisrael.org/bible-based-teaching-from-israel/blind-yet-seeing/

encouraging and inspirational. You, too, can minister right where you are. Your life can impact many. Your hands and feet can be like our Master Yeshua's, and even if you lack hands and feet, think of smiling Nick and his beautiful voice. There is great joy in ministering out of our weaknesses, for when we are weak, then we are strong. Paul said, "Therefore I am well content with weaknesses, with insults, with distresses, with persecutions, with difficulties, for Christ's sake; for when I am weak, then I am strong" (II Corinthians 12:10, NASB).

We have so much Time and so little to see. Strike that, now reverse it!

–Roald Dahl

PART 2

Review

1. Have you ever imagined yourself as a seed?

2. How do joy and purification come from suffering?

3. How much valuable time do we waste unaware?

4. Who are you mentoring right now with greatness inside them, things that need to be birthed for future generations?

5. How has reading the testimonies of Nick and Hellen encouraged you to minister with the gifts the Father has given you?

Jumping for Joy In the Midst of Sorrow

PART 3

Gobstoppers

And God said, "Behold, I have given you every plant yielding seed that is on the face of all the earth, and every tree with seed in its fruit. You shall have them for food.

–Genesis 1:29, ESV

The Bible lists many healthy foods and tips for healing. Song of Songs has various oils and healing properties associated with them, and Deuteronomy can also teach what foods there are to eat in a land that is good. Nonetheless, no matter what we do to stay fit and care for our temples, these temples will never walk through walls as our Messiah until "That Day," the day our Messiah returns, and we are redeemed. Paul confirms this: "Just as we have borne the image of the earthy, we will also bear the image of the heavenly" (I Corinthians 15:49, NASB). John tells us that when Messiah appears, we will be like Him because we will see the Messiah as He is. But until then, we have pain, suffering, and death. "For I consider that the sufferings of this present time are not worth comparing with the glory that is to be revealed to us" (Romans 8:18, ESV). Suffering and sorrow and despair are part of life.

Yes, until "That Day," pain comes in many forms. Some of us get a taste of multiple layers of pain. There is pain that causes our teeth to grind in our sleep. There's suffering that knocks the breath out of us--old age–creaking pain that bends backs over as our stature shrinks back towards the soil. We experience pain and chew our inner cheeks and nails down, pain that oozes out of our hearts like blood and stains our clothing. Pain that keeps our minds occupied in the night--pain due to stiff necks or bitterness. There is the pain of divorce, abandonment, losing loved ones, rejection, and the loss of a child. There is the pain of homelessness while living inside a house where no one communicates except through anger, silence, and unforgiveness. We have trauma triggers and soldiers suffering from wars, poverty, and so on. No one reading this is getting out alive. Pain shouts. Pain shrieks, it even roars, but there are treasures hidden inside of it. Yes, gems that require digging and searching.

> TV NEWSMAN: And now, details on the sudden announcement that has captured the attention of the entire world. Hidden among the countless billions of Wonka Bars are five gold tickets. And to the five people who find them will come the most fabulous prize one could wish for: a lifetime supply of chocolate.

Someday sweet as a song, Charlie's lucky day will come along. 'til that day, you've gotta stay in strong, Charlie. Up on top is right where you belong--look up Charlie, you'll see a star. Just follow it and keep your dream in view. Pretty soon, the sky is gonna clear up, Charlie. Cheer up, Charlie, do cheer up, Charlie. Just be glad you're you. [8]

–Roald Dahl

The wise men followed a star that led them to the Messiah. The same stars Abram looked up at. Abraham was told to count the stars if he could number them, and although Abraham's wife was old and barren, this would be the number of his seed. Abraham believed God, and it was credited to him as righteousness, but sometimes things become so hard, so dark, and so full of drudgery, it is hard to trust that Adonai sees us. One man named Job reminds us of such circumstances. Cheer up, Job, cheer up. Pretty soon, the sky is gonna clear up. Just be glad you're you, *Job.* In our story, the Creator of All will tell a man named Job sitting in ashes scraping his puss-filled sores with broken pottery to pray for his healthy friends. Job's pain had become a jawbreaker, a gobstopper, but the sky was getting ready to clear up. The book of Job is one of the most profound books in the Bible and the oldest one recorded. The Voice of

---

[8]

http://www.beckbackstage.org/uploads/3/4/1/0/34100493/tv_newsman_audition.pdf

Mighty (YHWH יהוה) thunders, and Job is catapulted straight up before the Holy One.

The Book of Job is an ancient piece of comparative theology and a deep well of wisdom to glean from. By the time Job, a blade of grass, a worm, stood before the Mighty King of Glory, he sees himself for the first time in the light of how small and insignificant his knowledge and understanding may be. Job, a man suffering horrendously, receives a stern message from the Holy One.

> Then the LORD answered Job from the whirlwind and said, "Now tighten the belt on your waist like a man; I will ask you, and you instruct Me. "Will you really nullify My judgment? Will you condemn Me so that you may be justified? "Or do you have an arm like God, And can you thunder with a voice like His?"
>
> –Job 40:6-9, NASB

Can you imagine what it would feel like to stand before the Holy One and hear the Voice of Thunder proclaim the message above while shaking in sackcloth and covered in sores? The length and depth of Job's sufferings are unthinkable and yet a comfort to us during our darkest journeys. In James' epistle, he tells us that Job is an example of how to endure trials. How did this man endure the loss of his children, servants, cattle, his health, and more?

> Job got up, tore his robe, and shaved his head; then he fell to the ground and worshiped. He said, "Naked I came from my mother's womb, And naked I shall return there. The LORD gave and the LORD has taken away. Blessed be the name of the LORD." Despite all this, Job did not sin, nor did he blame God.
>
> –Job 1:20-22, NASB

It is hard to measure our personal sufferings to those Job endured. There is one woman I want to highlight among Christian ministers. Her life and journey is a prime example of someone like Job. She has endured great hardships, and her story is an inspiration for us all. Her name is Joni.

Years ago, I watched a television show on a Christian network where a woman gave her testimony, and at the end of the show, the host wanted to pray for God to raise her up out of a wheelchair. She said, *"That's great; I'll take any prayers I can get but pray for my heart to be right. Pray for me to forgive quickly and to be used for His glory."* This is a paraphrase, but I never forgot Joni Eareckson Tada. When I think about Joni, my heart wants to burst. A teenager's dive into shallow water goes wrong. Joni suffered a fracture and became a quadriplegic (or tetraplegic), paralyzed from the shoulders down, but this woman with no ability to use her arms has written over 40 books. A golden ticket, Charlie!

Want to change the world? There's nothing to it.

–Roald Dahl

Back in the day, Joni learned to write with a pen and paint with a brush between her teeth. For me to list all her accomplishments and works would fill this room.

> Joni Tada Eareckson founded *Joni and Friends* in 1979, an organization to "accelerate Christian ministry in the disability community" throughout the world. In 2007 the Joni and Friends International Disability Center in Agoura Hills, California, was established. The Joni and Friends International Disability Center runs a multi-faceted non-profit covering a number of program outlets. The longest running program is *"Joni and Friends Radio"* and can be heard each weekday on over 1,000 broadcast outlets. Tada also records a one-minute radio broadcast *"Diamonds in the Dust,"* that airs daily. Other Joni and Friends programs include Family Retreats (a camp/retreat experience for families affected by disability), Wounded Warrior Getaways (which offer a similar experience for families of Wounded Warriors), and Wheels for the World (collects manual wheelchairs and other mobility devices which are refurbished by volunteers in prison restoration shops then shipped

overseas where the wheelchairs are fitted by physical therapists to people in developing nations). [9]

—Wikipedia

What would possess a person to help so many suffering souls? What would cause a person to refurbish wheelchairs and support wounded warriors? Another wounded warrior--a diamond in the dust, Joni could have wallowed in pity and defeat, but she has acquired extraordinary accomplishments while running her race to get the gold. Her paintings and words help heal many who walk upright and use hands and feet and limbs that work perfectly. She is running even though she cannot stand.

> Grandpa Joe: *I never thought my life could be anything but catastrophe. but suddenly I begin to see a bit of good luck for me cause I've got a golden ticket. I've got a golden twinkle in my eye. I never had a chance to shine. never a happy song to sing. but suddenly half the world is mine. what an amazing thing cause I've got a golden ticket.*

—Roald Dahl

How does the story of Job end?

The Lord restored the fortunes of Job when he prayed for his friends, and the Lord increased all that Job had

---
[9] https://en.wikipedia.org/wiki/Joni_Eareckson_Tada

twofold. Then all his brothers and all his sisters and all who had known him before came to him, and they ate bread with him in his house; and they consoled him and comforted him for all the adversities that the Lord had brought on him.

–Job 42:10-11, NASB

Job's life was a Gobstopper, but now the Holy One has brought restoration. During Job's trials, we read, "In all this, Job did not sin or charge God with wrongdoing" (Job 1:22, BSB). The Everlasting Gobstopper is a type of candy from Roald Dahl's 1964 children's novel *Willy Wonka and the Chocolate Factory*. A young poverty-stricken boy named Charlie is tested. Slugworth, the movies main antagonist, promised riches for stealing Wonka's everlasting gobstopper candy, but this was nothing more than an illusion. As it turned out, the gobstopper was a ploy to test Charlie's loyalty and nobility. Charlie did not know that he was being tested. Many times we are not aware either. Slugworth attempts to bribe the children visiting the Wonka factory to steal one Gobstopper for him. This is later revealed as a lie; Slugworth is one of Wonka's workers. The proposal is a test Wonka set up to judge the worthiness of the ticket holders to take over the factory. "Upon being handed back the metaphoric candy from Charlie, Wonka utters, "*so shines a good deed in a weary world.*"

We are tested in many things during this life, even difficult illnesses, losses, and mental anguish. The life of Job and Joni give us much to ponder. Their lives are examples for all of us during times of testing. Peter tells us not to be surprised at the fiery trial that comes our way. "In this you rejoice, though now for a little while, if necessary, you have been grieved by various trials, so that the tested genuineness of your faith—more precious than gold that perishes though it is tested by fire—may be found to result in praise and glory and honor at the revelation of Jesus Christ" (I Peter 1:6-7, ESV). May the Father restore us. May Adonai use our teeth, our ears, our eyes, and every part of our body that will function for His purposes. Let us find joy and courage amid our sufferings. May we, like Job, pray for our friends while we are in dire need of miracles. Sing with me, Cheer up, Charlie, cheer up. Look to the heavens, and soon you will see a star. Life is full of golden tickets, my friends, do not lose heart amid sorrow, for there is joy that is being birthed through it.

PART 3

Review

1. A woman named Joni, with no arms, has written over 40 books. How does her journey inspire you?

2. Abraham believed God even though it looked impossible. What are you believing Him for today?

3. Have you ever read the book of Job in its entirety? What did you learn?

4. How do you endure trials?

5. How can we acquire vision for a future glory amid our sufferings?

SECTION # 4

Joy is Sitting Right Next to Sorrow

The next three devotionals showcase the precious joy we often receive after the pain, the death, and the hopelessness.

> *When Jesus rose from prayer and returned to the disciples, He found them asleep, exhausted from sorrow.*
> *–Luke 22:45, BSB*

Jumping for Joy In the Midst of Sorrow

PART 1

Hope Deferred

What can be learned from situations that seem bleak or hopeless? Perhaps there is a reason tucked inside the changing tide that is higher than our human understanding? Joy can come from the darkest of places and ignite like a sparkler in the blackest sky.

In my early 20s, this suburbia girl found herself living in a shotgun house with ceiling tiles missing, windows nailed shut, and a dark alley that allowed one to park right up to the back door and jolt inside for safety. The shingles slid off the roof like a sleigh in winter and landed next to the chipped army green porch. My mind could not comprehend how a young woman like myself, raised in a quiet subdivision, had ended up with a box of government cheese and several mouths to feed. In the past, my prior husband and I had lived off and on with my father-in-law. We had lived with my brother, my sister, and sometimes we just struggled to live. But the year or two I spent in this place taught me more life lessons than I could have imagined. It was primarily due to my next-door neighbor.

She had one of those cool unisex names you hear spoken over a spunky three-year-old tomboy with ringlets--a name like Charlie, Jessie, and Bobbie. I'll call her Johnnie. The first time I met Johnnie is imprinted in my mind, branded even. I had just moved into a house on the other side of the railroad tracks. You know, the side where the white folks turn honey brown and the corner store sells more lottery tickets and liquor than food. My neighborhood was not frequented by family much, and my mother refused to visit in her sports car after my car was vandalized. The trunk busted open. The windows shattered. The small home had one air conditioning unit and several rooms with slanted floors, paneling from 1950, and dirt for a yard, which saved us gas in the mower. For months, we had a refrigerator but no stove. For cooking purposes, I used an electric skillet to supplement the microwave. The dark paneled walls left much to be desired, and, unbeknownst to me, there was a rat infestation in the building at the end of my backyard.

One night, in the summer of 1991, I was hot and slightly pregnant with my third son, a gift from above. I had gone outside to sit on the porch and look up at the moon, feel the breeze blow upon my perspiring neck, and try to cool off a bit. As I sat there, a man approached me and began to talk smack. He made sexual advances. His eyes were shifting up and down, and then his words began to make me nervous. He was darker than honey brown—warm charcoal. It would be hours before my then-husband would be home from his second job delivering pizzas. I could not breathe. I eyed the distance from the steps by the sidewalk to my front door. My children were sleeping. Suddenly out of nowhere, Johnnie was standing behind the man, and swifter than a jackrabbit, she jumped up and grabbed his arm. I heard the click of her switchblade before I listened to her voice that bellowed, "Nigga, touch this girl, and I'll kill ya. I'll drain your blood all over the sidewalk. Understand? Now get on outta here." I watched the man stagger on down the sidewalk, mouthing words unheard of in my familiar circles.

I looked up at this savior--this woman who was smiling from ear to ear and began to thank her and explain how I wasn't sure what I would have done if she hadn't come along at just the right time. However, my eyes were carefully watching the knife and her hands that folded and slid it back down into her front pocket. She smiled even wider, her gold front tooth catching the streetlight.

"Girl, he knows better than to mess with Johnnie Portland! You saw his tired @##% get on down the street didn't ya. Ha Ha! My name's Johnnie, and you must be my new neighbor. Yep, that's my little house next door."

She pointed to the brown shotgun house on the left side of me with pride. She held her arms out and hugged me. I will never forget that moment. It was a hug with several layers of good fat. The kind of fat that smells like cornbread and greens, fried chicken, and biscuits made with real butter. Her body grabbed me and enveloped me in a sandwich-style hold. "Anyone around here tries and mess with you just call ol' Johnnie. I'll make sure you're okay. Alright? Alright then, shoot. You don't really need to be out here at night alone, though. Understand?" I nodded, smiled, and tilted my head down nervously, then back up again. "Girl, you're not from around here, are ya?" "No, I must admit, I'm not. Thanks for looking out for me."

In the summer of 1991, Johnnie taught me lessons I would never learn at a college or a church house. Like the time I had to gas up for work on an early Sunday morning and was confronted by a drunk man, reeking and slurring. From the sight of him, he had been in a fight. There was blood and cuts on his dress shirt and hand. He did not look homeless. He had a nice suit coat and dress pants on. He tried to grab my purse and began asking for my money. I looked him directly in the eye, and, in Johnnie fashion, said, "I don't have any money, and I'm on my way to work. Now go inside and clean yourself up. You're drunk." He looked stunned but headed towards the door of the corner store. He had obeyed me like the man Johnnie had told to get on down the road.

Somehow, I had moved to this area of town and reached this place of loss and poverty through events that caused a chain reaction. I was uneducated, pregnant with a third, and at times depressed. Johnnie helped me get through many social issues and spiritual issues. She had a way of making me believe and hope. My place of poverty was her place of rescue. It was her new beginning. Her vision was helping me adjust to the news lens my eyes were taking in. Could I find gratitude in this place I had landed?

I will never forget the first time I was invited to Johnnie's house and ushered into her living room. She smiled her fantastic smile while taking off her flip-flop to swat a cockroach that she declared was just greeting me at the door. As I made my way into the kitchen, I met her son and daughter, who were both pleasant and excited to get to know me--their mysterious new neighbor. Johnnie was wearing a housecoat, and she had a comb stuck in her hair. She had spunk and big, beautiful eyes. Jonnie also had a huge cast-iron skillet. She was carefully and meticulously frying up chicken Colonel Sanders would have coveted. Her daughter squashed a roach and looked at me, and made a face. "I hate these bugs, mama," she said. "I'm scared they will crawl inside my ears while I'm asleep, or worse my mouth." I shook my head and said how sorry I was, while trying to refrain from leaping atop the table and screaming for the Orkin man to come and fumigate the place.

Johnnie brushed it off and acted as if she was not aware of the roaches that greeted her guest. Instead, she ushered me back into the front room and began to show off her new black sofa and love seat. "I got this living room furniture at Rent-A-Center. Just got rid of my tired raggedy little couch last week." She pointed to her new glass coffee table and bragged. Johnnie was taking me on a tour of her little house like many who live in mansions would do. She loved it here. It was much better than the last place Jonnie had lived. "We hardly ever hear any gunshots," she said. I sighed, thinking about the sights and sounds of my new environment. It was finally starting to sink in. I had been thrust into a social status that was unfamiliar. At the ripe age of 24, I had felt eviction, gone without electricity, scrounged for food, and watched my husband turn the water back on from the main shut off. However, now I had entered a place different from my childhood. I didn't understand the culture or language, but thank the Lord, I had a friend. This friend would help me survive, make me smile, love me for who I was, and cause my children's eyes to light up every time she made an appearance.

One night, I told Johnnie that we should go to the store and get bombs to let off and kill all the roaches. I told her I needed some as well and would share with her. Even though I lacked ceilings and a stove, I had not seen any roaches. We carted her kids off to spend the night with family and sealed up the windows. The next morning after sweeping up the dead bugs and cleaning the floors, I was thanked by her daughter, who told me she thought she would find it easier to sleep now. A few months later, I asked her son and daughter what color they would like their rooms to be painted. The young man wanted blue. He was named after the great Italian poet, Dante Alighieri, but I was not sure he, nor his mother who placed the title on him, knew this. Honestly, I did not at the time. This was before taking art history and English 101 years later. Her daughter wanted a pink or purple room, like most girls her age. Johnnie and I got to work the following week painting their rooms.

One morning, after another bombing of bugs, Johnnie sent her daughter over to get me. She was frying country steaks, crispy potatoes, and making buttery biscuits. "I've got plenty," she said. I noticed a bottle of bleach and a mop and began to clean and sweep up dead roaches. I pressed the bleach-filled mop hard against the linoleum until its dark sticky brown turned a speckled robin blue. Johnnie's husband came in from the bedroom to the kitchen and looked as surprised to see a white gal mopping his floor as he did the blue color that had laid dormant underneath. He smiled and said, "Wow, it looks nice in here." Johnnie introduced us. He grabbed his food and kissed his woman and then made his way back down the hall where he would collide on the mattress in front of the small TV. Johnnie's kids ran from their rooms to the kitchen, back and forth bringing me pictures they had colored and school papers which they were proud of. Her young son had won a creative writing contest for budding authors. Maybe she knew more about his famous name than I had given her credit.

My children ended up playing with her children and their cousins. Some people warned me to keep my sons away from the children there, but what harm could come from children running through dirt, kicking balls, and passing the hours away with make-believe games? Were we different from them? No, and our children found ways amid poverty to laugh, hide, run, play, and eat their share of cold leftover pizzas. No color or prejudice mindset came between us. Each skin pigment was a beautiful hue of copper and gold, coffee and cream, and respect.

Johnnie knew about life, and she knew about death. She had lost family to senseless drugs, and, yes, shots fired. One night, Johnnie pointed to each house on the street, and one by one, informed me of who lived there. She knew who was hooked on crack or some other substance. Johnnie knew who was a God-fearing man and who was a nosey woman. She knew the names of the dirty kids that lived on the corner. Whenever they came to her house, she would give them baths because she never knew if they had water or not. Johnnie was cleaning things more important than floors.

Dinners were shared between our two families on many nights, and her food stamps supplied a few staple items when things were lean for my family. One night after Johnnie had bought a lottery ticket, she looked at me and said, "When I win the lottery, I am going to get off these little food stamps." I said, "Well, Johnnie, with millions you could eat dinner in a different country every night." She had no idea what a million dollars even amounted to. Like me, she lacked math skills but not love. She brought me half of her government cheese, and I gave her half my towels I found at a yard sale. She got my boys' soda pops and Cheetos and hugged them in Johnnie fashion. I helped her children with homework. When the day came that I went into labor, Johnnie came over and cleaned my house. She folded my clothes and picked up the toys. When my relatives and family members showed up to see the baby, they were quite surprised to see Johnnie embracing my Samuel in a motherly hold. Her eyes lit up as she looked down at my son like he was part of her. Anytime she came by to visit, she would walk in and look me in the eye, that gold tooth shining, and exclaim, "Give me my Lil white baby!"

Over the years, we lost touch. I moved, then she moved. Gosh, I loved her, and how I miss her. I wonder if her son is writing. I wonder if her daughter is a mother now. I can still taste her chicken, her words, and her heart. She forever changed my view of the world and my voice as a writer. Wherever you are tonight, Johnnie, thank you for saving me on a hot summer night and for sharing all your wealth with me. Your wealth was what helped me get through many rough nights. And when I packed up and moved back across town into a lower-middle-class subdivision, the smallest unkempt house on the street, I was ecstatic. Every room had ceilings, and the backyard was fenced in. There were no dilapidated buildings with rats or mice—no bugs greeting friends at the door. The backyard had a bright green substance called grass, and the front porch was safe enough to sit on most nights at any hour and gaze up at the moon. However, no one brought me or my children golden smiles, packaged cheese, and hope the size of giant helium balloons.

Whatever you are going through right now that looks hopeless and without joy, just remember joy comes in multiple hues and often gives us lessons we would never choose, but underneath the poverty is a wealth of knowledge. Praise Him for where you are, for Joseph would have never acquired the tools he needed for the palace if he had not ventured to the pit and the prison.

PART 1

Review

1. Who in your life has affected you as Johnnie influenced my life?

2. What wisdom can we acquire by being thrust out of our comfort zone?

3. Define poverty in a spiritual sense? "For you say, I am rich, I have prospered, and I need nothing, not realizing that you are wretched, pitiable, poor, blind, and naked. I counsel you to buy from me gold refined by fire, so that you may be rich, and white garments so that you may clothe yourself and the shame of your nakedness may not be seen, and salve to anoint your eyes, so that you may see" (Revelations 3:17-18, ESV).

4. Do you believe the Father orders our steps? If so, can you see His Hand at work even if your surroundings look different than you imagined?

5. Who has impacted your life in a way similar to Johnnie and her ability to make me see the glass half full?

PART 2

Long Suffering

Take a moment and meditate on your life--the day of your birth, your parents, your geographical place of landing--siblings, gifting, and the era you are living in. Now, picture yourself from a heavenly perspective, a tiny dot on the globe. Like a pebble thrown into the river, we send ripples into the world. Our words, smiles, laughter, tears, trauma, heartbreak, and incredible moments are interconnected, creating us as individuals with different experiences. Yet, we are all more alike than we realize. How do we deal with suffering, fear, sorrow, and pain? How do we experience joy, the gladness of heart, and become content as the Apostle Paul in all circumstances?

> Not that I speak from want, for I have learned to be content in whatever circumstances I am. I know how to get along with humble means, and I also know how to live in prosperity; in any and every circumstance I have learned the secret of being filled and going hungry, both

of having abundance and suffering need. I can do all things through Him who strengthens me.

–Philippians 4:11-13, NASB

Paul learned contentment that only comes from above. He rejoices even in his suffering.

Long-suffering is something we do, not just something we experience. Much of the fruits of the spirit have to do with actions. The Hebrew word *simchah* is the word most often translated as *joy* in our Bibles, and it is almost always expressed through our actions. Joy happens to us as we go through life, but joy comes from trusting the Father and having peace even during great trials. We are told in Galatians about the fruit of the Spirit. This fruit resides on one tree, and amid words like love, joy, and peace, we find long-suffering. How many of us rejoice in our sufferings? Paul tells us to do just that: "And not only this, but we also celebrate in our tribulations, knowing that tribulation brings about perseverance;" (Romans 5:3, NASB).

Many persons suffering today will run to the doctor for a quick fix. They want to numb the process. For hard difficult work, debt, health, family issues, then doctors say, "Take this antidepressant, and you will not have to experience this long-suffering or depressive state." They may not inform us that we will not experience the joy either. Antidepressants numb a person's emotions. Our emotions work together. We cannot feel joy when we are numb to all our feelings. I once was put on antidepressants, and if my house was on fire, I would have sat peacefully and watched it burn. Even hugging my sons felt robotic. In Hebrew thought, everything has feelings. The rocks cry out. The trees clap their hands. The mountains burst into song. Everything is alive. Dead people feel nothing. Yeshua said, "Let the dead bury their own dead. You, however, go and proclaim the kingdom of God" (Luke 9:60, NASB).

Some of my greatest joy came after intense suffering and devastation. After losing my home and all my possessions, a year later, I opened the door to an apartment that was 600 square feet. and bowed on my knees with great joy. I laid my face in the carpeting and bawled, weeping, and praising the Father with unspeakable joy. I felt emotions I had never felt. I could control my thermostat, turn a knob and get water, and drink from my own coffee cup in the serenity of a space chalked out for me. The smallest space I had ever occupied was peaceful. I owned nothing but a bed and a couch: no silverware, no sweeper, no pots and pans, dishes, furniture, or accessories. My brother was able to fit everything I owned on his truck, yet there was magnificent joy in that small space. There were songs of praise and dancing of feet. I met my husband there. I healed from much brokenness there. I was blessed with provision to buy new items that were a representation of the new things the Father was doing in my life. While still traveling through homelessness and heartbreak, He kept whispering one verse to my spirit—one verse that seemed impossible to envision until it came forth. "Behold, I am doing a new thing; now it springs forth, do you not perceive it?" (Isaiah 43:19, ESV). But what if I would have never experienced being homeless and just moved from my lovely home to this tiny space with people above me and beside me? The walls were thin, and it was not abnormal to hear my neighbor cooking, showering, or listening to the television. If I had not lost everything beforehand, would I have had such gratitude for my tiny space? Doubtful. "Weeping may last for the night, But a shout of joy comes in the morning" (Psalms 30:5, NASB). Paul explains what is happening to our outward shell and our inward spirit.

> Therefore we do not lose heart, but though our outer man is decaying, yet our inner man is being renewed day by day. For momentary, light affliction is producing for us an eternal weight of glory far beyond all comparison.
>
> –II Corinthians 4:16-17, NASB

A person who has suffered a long time often needs to speak of strange symptoms and pain. They need to vent, describing it to those willing to share in their suffering, but if great testimony came forth from that dark place, they have the ability to offer hope to a person walking through a dark period or strange situation. Most of the people I know who have compassion and a willing ear have suffered for a season--long-suffering.

There is nothing quite as painful as sitting in a room in horrific pain or feeling depressed. We listen as those around us talk, share, and laugh. Even worse is being cooped up in a hospital bed or nursing home with no one talking at all. In these seasons, we try and appear normal for the sake of family, friends, or the nurses, but often our body or our mind is screaming, "Don't you know what I am going through?" These are words we may wish to speak, but instead, we ask for water or inquire about our friend's new hairstyle. We count the minutes on the clock and wait for someone, anyone to see we are silently dying inside.

Another cruelty is having someone tell us not to speak of our long-suffering. They quote, 'life and death are in the power of the tongue" (Proverbs 18:21, BSB). But denying pain in any form, will not make the pain go away. Vulnerability and openness can bring empathy, and prayer. The shepherd David did not say the giant Goliath did not exist. " Then David said to the Philistine, " This day the LORD will deliver you into my hand, and I will strike you down and cut off your head" (I Samuel 17:46, ESV). If our child were to cut off his arm, would we just tell him to say that his arm was whole—envision his arm whole? Meanwhile, he is bleeding out. No. Of course not. We need to be more like David, who had a different spirit. When he saw the giant, no alarm went off inside his soul because he believed in a God bigger than any giant. When we experience trials that appear to be gigantic, we must trust in the One who parted the sea, raised the dead, feeds the birds, and dresses the flowers in more glory than king Solomon.

If you have a loved one battling depression, divorce, the loss of a child, a chronic illness, give that person space to heal. Try not to use words like "Snap out of it. You just need to go for a walk, get some sunlight, or heaven needed another angel and that's why God took your child." Depression can be crueler than physical pain. I cannot imagine the loss of a child, and multiple experiences of injustices and trauma are often so grievous that we would all do well to sit in silence. Even Job's friends started out with great compassion.

> When they lifted up their eyes at a distance and did not recognize him, they raised their voices and wept. And each of them tore his robe and they threw dust over their heads toward the sky. Then they sat down on the ground with him for seven days and seven nights with no one speaking a word to him, for they saw that his pain was very great.
>
> –Job 2:12-13, NASB

The Book of Proverbs warns what not to do around those who are troubled. "Like one who takes off a garment on a cold day, or like vinegar on soda, Is he who sings songs to a troubled heart" (Proverbs 25:20, NASB).

The good news is trees can bear beautiful fruit, and long-suffering is only one fruit. There is also love, joy, peace, kindness, goodness, faithfulness, gentleness, and self-control. I pray that whatever you are going through at this moment has a greater reward, and that you, too, are rejoicing in the endurance of the race you are running. Run the race to get the prize. Remember, out of great suffering comes great joy. He may be changing your life in some way as He did in Joseph's, and possibly you are unable to see the end result of yet.

PART 2

Review

1. The fruit that comes from long-suffering is often not seen until afterward. How has long-suffering brought joy into your life?

2. When you are suffering, do you try and numb the experience? If so, how?

3. When was the last time you felt content?

4. How does suffering teach endurance?

5. Can you see the Father changing your life due to the trials you have experienced?

PART 3

Friends That Shine Like the Son

Some memories sneak up on us at different seasons. One particular visit to some dear friends years ago is a memory I will always cherish. Cheri and her husband Wade are people who have impacted my life. I love Cheri's heart and her missionary work in poverty-stricken countries. Cheri does not have much money, but what extra she does have, she uses to buy Bibles for orphans in Malawi or put a roof on a church that literally has an open heaven with rain coming inside. Most of us would not walk a mile to sit in a building in the rain with no roof. The people in Malawi are hungry in more ways than one.

Cheri shared with me how she collected money for one of the tin roofs in Malawi and how the people lined up when she got out of the car. They were in such awe of the blessing; they were crying tears of gratitude. The people were running to honor her. One Malawian woman gave her a royal gift, a chicken. Cheri's husband, Wade, was diagnosed with ALS shortly before my husband and I met them for the first time. On one particular day, I made a meal to bring with us in the car because Wade could no longer get out of the house due to his health. We laughed and ate and talked and prayed. It was Shabbat, and as I watched my friend feed her husband his taco, I wondered what it was like for her to hand feed her spouse. The movies usually depict a star-struck couple feeding each other seductively with chocolate-covered strawberries, but what is it like to look into the eyes of the one you are one with and realize that each moment is sacred. Each smile. Each wipe of a cheek.

Cheri's shoulders are pillars, and her legs are firmly planted. She is like a strong tree—a woman of valor. Cheri was exhausted that day, but a stranger would never have known it. After a bit of visiting and eating, I sat with her husband Wade on his enclosed patio. He rode in his wheelchair, and I followed. I plopped down on a cushioned seat and admired the beach theme of furnishings, and petted his dog, Tutt. After a moment, Wade said, "I like to sit out here in the mornings and look outside. The sun cascades through the window and shines on my legs and my face."

On this day, Wade had not been able to leave his home for months. As he spoke, I remembered a time, shortly after my release of *Walter the Homeless Man*, when I had been to Mayo clinic and was extremely ill. There had been much stress and family matters that seemed to take me over the edge. I had to stay in bed upstairs at our old house, and my husband had to make sure I had water, medication, and snacks– everything I would need because I could not get up and down the steps while he was at work. I was much too weak. A few weeks later, and a few rounds of IV steroids, I was able to take a car ride to a restaurant called The Overlook–Walter's Pub. Walter's Pub has floor-length glass windows on a hillside overlooking the water. It was fall, and all the leaves had changed from green to a beautiful golden orange that lit up the sky. I was weak, but, oh, so thankful to be out of bed. I cried most of the way there—tears of joy. Have you ever cried over the color of the leaves? Have you ever cried over the sun shining on your face?

I love the Father, and I would not trade a minute of the journey– as Garth Brooks bellows in my head– "I could have missed the pain, but I'd a had to miss the dance." Every day and especially during a pandemic, it can be easy to overlook His beauty and All of His wondrous creation. It is easy to complain about our situations. My friend with ALS never complained that day. Wade, a once strong carpenter, a trade of our Master and Savior, had gained some different tools in his toolbox. These tools taught me many lessons, and as the evening drew near, he struggled to cough. After composing himself, Wade continued to smile and joke about the ball game. He spoke about how good it felt to sit in his recliner since my husband was there to help him in and out of it. He was enjoying the day. The Shabbat in all her Glory was shining on him. My friend Wade did not lament about a whole host of things--tiny things you and I might take for granted, like small organs that lay hidden behind ribs and bones that one day will come together and stand dressed in glory, but for now, each day, my friend grows worse, yet stronger. I am reminded of the Apostle Paul's words.

> And He has said to me, "My grace is sufficient for you, for power is perfected in weakness." Most gladly, therefore, I will rather boast about my weaknesses, so that the power of Christ may dwell in me. Therefore I am well content with weaknesses, with insults, with distresses, with persecutions, with difficulties, for Christ's sake; for when I am weak, then I am strong.
>
> –II Corinthians 12:9-10, NASB

Meeting these two friends has been one of the biggest blessings in my husband and my life. They are people of integrity, and one day I'll dance with Wade, and we will have a drink of the best wine ever tasted–poured out by the greatest Servant that has ever walked this earth, Yeshua.

Shortly after writing this devotional chapter, our dear friend Wade passed away at the exact moment the Lamb of God, who takes away the sins of the world, did. It was Passover at around 3 pm. We are thankful Wade is no longer suffering and that one day we will see him again. Each morning presents new obstacles and new sunrises — new colors of paint. Today, Yeshua Messiah's Spirit lives in us, and we are said to have the same mind as our

Messiah. May we try harder to reflect His foliage. Yes, let us work harder to have compassion for the hurting. See the trees for the first time. Taste the rain when we are sick of it. Make a snow angel as a child would. Notice the people Adonai places in front of us. Feel the sun's warmth and sing to the moon, for time is speeding faster, and each day the mirror shows we have grown older–weaker. Let us give Glory for our breath in the morning. May we become more forgiving–more steadfast. Guard our hearts against those who would cause us to dwell on things that are toxic and meaningless. Everything can be taken from us in an instant.

"Moses, today you are going to walk up a hill and die. Take this cup from me, Yeshua cried. "Take this cup!" Our Messiah said Father, not my will but Yours be done.

This life is such an incredible journey. No matter how long we are here, each day is like putty in our hands, a paintbrush between our teeth, a golden ticket, a song, and we can feed a hungry child naturally or spiritually. We can collect money for a roof, notice the sun shining on our face, the color of the leaves, or the bareness of a tree waiting to bud for the next season. Even a tree that looks dead has sap bubbling up underneath, just waiting to blossom and bloom. My prayer for you is that you taste this joy and dance in it. Many times, there is brightness and the glory of all His Creation right in front of our faces, but we cannot see it. Our focus must change for this joy to bubble up and renew our strength. Today, wherever you are, whatever you are going through, taste and see that He is good, for He is a good, good Father.

PART 3

Review

1. Have you ever cried over the color of the leaves or the sun shining on your face?

2. What gratitude can be learned through suffering?

3. It seems that many times the very ones suffering give more to the orphans, widows, and poor than those with great wealth and great health. Why do you think this is?

4. In Luke 14, we read about a banquet and invitations. How does the dinner guest change, and why?

But He said to him, "A man was giving a big dinner, and he invited many; and at the dinner hour he sent his slave to tell those who had been invited, 'Come, because everything is ready now.' And yet they all alike began to make excuses. The first one said to him, 'I purchased a field and I need to go out to look at it; please consider me excused.' And another one said, 'I bought five yoke of oxen, and I am going to try them out; please consider me excused.' And another one said, 'I took a woman as my wife, and for that reason I cannot come.' And the slave came back and reported this to his master. Then the head of the household became angry and said to his slave, 'Go out at once into the streets and lanes of the city and bring in here those who are poor, those with disabilities, those who are blind, and those who are limping.' And later the slave said, 'Master, what you commanded has been done, and still there is room.' And the master said to the slave, 'Go out into the roads and the hedges and press upon them to come in, so that my house will be filled. For I tell you, none of those men who were invited shall taste my dinner.'"

–Luke 14:16-24, NASB

5. If you had to name your favorite fragrance, what would it be? What symbolism can we learn from the crushing of flowers and our own perfume?

SECTION # 5

Son Flower Seeds

The next three devotionals bring shouts of Joy to those who are weary, bearing precious seeds.

> *He who goes out weeping, bearing a trail of seed, will surely return with shouts of joy, carrying sheaves of grain.*
>
> *– Psalm 126:6, BSB*

Jumping for Joy In the Midst of Sorrow

PART 1

The Potter's House

On the day of prosperity be happy, But on the day of adversity consider: God has made the one as well as the other So that a person will not discover anything that will come after him.

–Ecclesiastes 7:14, NASB

We are thrown into situations at times that are so disparaging that we cannot see an end to the turmoil. We long for joy and envision how we want things to work out in our lives, but what if the suffering is causing a more profound purpose? What if the pain is like a tree's pruning or the potter's wheel with its spinning, shaping, and molding? What if our suffering is for a greater good and has something to do with our calling? Joseph's training required years of testing and trials, all meant for a greater good. Many times, the suffering we experience leaves us unable to sleep. We are wide awake physically, but spiritually we may be sleepwalking.

If you were a god who wanted to wake people up, who would you send to do that job? John came as a voice. Prophets are not born; they are built. John was a High Priest and a prophet. We, His humble servants, teachers, and ministers of His Word, are not just born equipped. We are thrown on His wheel. This wheel is spinning round and round while the clay is being reshaped, molded, and tossed. The throwing, slapping, and shaping of a lump of clay can be painful. It is placed centrally on the wheel and then squeezed, lifted, and shaped as the wheel turns. Our lives can mimic this process.

> Then I {Jeremiah} went down to the Potter's house, and there he was making something on the wheel. But the vessel that he was making of clay was spoiled in the hand of the Potter; so he remade it into another vessel, as it pleased the potter to make.
>
> –Jeremiah 18:2-4, NASB

Soft clay can be smacked and thrown down on the potter's wheel and reshaped. Once the pot is fired, it is a whole different story. The Father told Jeremiah that He knew him before He placed him in the womb and called him to be a prophet to the nations, but Jeremiah was built. Most are familiar with a verse that says, "Your mercies are made new each morning," but what was the prophet speaking before all this? He was talking to a people who had not been obedient and had gone whoring. Jeremiah may have been describing the curses that had overtaken Yahweh's people due to their sins and their lack of keeping His Sabbaths, His Commandments, and caring for the orphans and widows. The Father of glory was weeping for His Bride. The book of Lamentations is read on the 9th of Av. The 9th of Av is said to be when the spies returned with an evil report except for Caleb and Joshua. "The First Temple was destroyed on the 9th of Av (423 BCE). Five centuries later (in 69 CE), as the Romans drew closer to the Second Temple, ready to torch it, the Jews were shocked to realize that their Second Temple was destroyed the same day as the first. [10]

To include all the tragedies said to have happened on this date would take quite a bit of time. Even World War One occurred on the 9th of Av. By the time we get to the gas chambers and Hitler, to collect the Jewish people's tears would have taken bottles that could hold a whole ocean of waters. Lamentations begins with the Hebrew word *Eicha* which means *how*? It is a prophetic response to the destruction of the temple in 586 B.C.E. We also are temples that at times must destruct so that the Lord can breathe new life into us. The prophet Jeremiah's words in the Biblical book of Lamentations are poignant and heart-wrenching.

> He bent His bow And took aim at me as a target for the arrow. He made the arrows of His quiver Enter my inward

---

[10] https://www.chabad.org/library/article_cdo/aid/946703/jewish/What-Happened-on-the-Ninth-of-Av.htm

parts. I have become a laughingstock to all my people, Their song of ridicule all the day. He has filled me with bitterness, He has made me drink plenty of wormwood. He has also made my teeth grind with gravel; He has made me cower in the dust. My soul has been excluded from peace; I have forgotten happiness.

–Lamentations 3:12-17, NASB

As sons and daughters, we will be shaped on the potter's wheel. Who is man to think that he is the one who can form the clay?

Woe to the one who quarrels with his Maker—A piece of pottery among the other earthenware pottery pieces! Will the clay say to the potter, 'What are you doing?' Or the thing you are making say, 'He has no hands'?

–Isaiah 45:9, NASB

According to scripture, our Yeshua Messiah was placed on that potter's wheel. He learned obedience through suffering: "Although He was a Son, He learned obedience from the things which He suffered" (Hebrews 5:8, NASB). As servants of Adonai, we are thrown on the Potter's wheel. The prophets experienced intense suffering. Most of the prophets could relate to Jeremiah's lament. They had been through just about everything one could think or imagine. Elijah arrives on the scene, and we read nothing much about his background. He boldly confronts kings and commands the sky to stay shut and slaughters hundreds of the false prophets of Baal. How did Elijah and others get such tenacity? I will tell you. It was not by being pampered and coddled. Prophets were fearful of the call. The prophets pointed out their weaknesses with fear when called. They said things like, "I can't speak. I am too young. I am the least in my father's house. I am a fig farmer. I stutter." They knew where prophets went. It was usually to oppose a priest—a king—a wicked leader with a booming voice from Adonai and then off to the prison, death, a cave, a lion's den. Prophets were built to confront those no one else wanted to face—stiff-necked people—like an Ahab or a Jezebel. The Father whispered in the ear of Nathan words that would make even strong men shudder. Nathan go tell my servant David, the one who carried Goliath, the giant's head on a pole, that he is the man who has sinned against me. Because of the magnitude of the call concerning the prophets, and the weight of the assignments, we hear them proclaim as Jeremiah did that he was too young to speak or as Moses who professed to stutter. They knew what type of call this was.

The burden of the word of the Lord Adonai—that's how the prophet's letters began. It is a burden to feel what the Father feels. It is a burden to see what the Father sees. How does a loving Father develop a man or woman with no regard for whether people will like the sound of the words they use? How does one form a person on a potter's wheel who does not care if their message from HaShem causes one to never speak to them again? HaShem was developing a man or woman who could deliver a message from Him, even if it cost them their lives like Stephen,

John the Baptist, and Paul. What ingredients go into the batter to prepare such a person? Possibly the Potter wants such an individual to be shunned by those esteemed--the ones in the important circles. How does Adonai build and shape a vessel that will speak what He tells them to speak even if their closest friends and companions walk away? Perhaps He causes them to be loved by people who they love with so much love it bubbles up inside their soul, and then He allows those same people to reject, crush, and defame their character and trust. Yeshua asked His disciples, "Are you able to drink the cup that I am about to drink?" (Matthew 20:22, NASB). The cup is raised, but can we drink such bitterness, suffering, and death? Our hearts often speak as Peter's did. "Even though all may fall away because of You, I will never fall away." Jesus said to him, "Truly, I say to you that this very night before a rooster crows, you will deny Me three times." Peter said to Him, "Even if I have to die with You, I will not deny You." All the disciples said the same thing too" (Matthew 26:33-35, NASB). All the sheep scatter and run in fear during Yeshua's darkest time of suffering. Many times, those closest to us do the same. Sometimes the Father allows it so that we will draw closer to Him. Sometimes we must fear the burden.

How do you build, form, and shape a person so that they have no concern for material things? No regard for money or titles? No affection for the esteem of man? You strip them of everything they own. You cause them to live by a brook and let ravens feed them as they fed Elijah the prophet. You send them to a widow with a few drops of oil and a handful of flour. You leave them naked and bare, and they see all the material as worthless. Mother Teresa could not be bought—she had her eyes on a different prize. Mother Teresa began missionary work with the poor in 1948. She was alone. She had no one to help her--no friends and no money. Teresa Bojaxhiu picked up a stick, and before a group of curious children who had never seen the inside of a schoolhouse, she began to write the Bengali alphabet on the ground in the dust with a stick. [11]

The apostles could not be bought. Saints do not store up treasures on earth that cannot bring joy. Earthly treasures are just objects that collect dust. The pricier the objects, the more concern we have of thieves stealing these possessions. Those who die in Yeshua cannot be bought or enticed by men. "But Jesus, on His part, was not entrusting Himself to them, for He knew all men, and because He did not need anyone to testify concerning man, for He Himself knew what was in man" (John 2:23-24, NASB).

Following the imagery of the Master Potter molding and shaping us on His wheel using His Hands, tools, and Word, Our Potter, the Ancient of Days, has a plan for us. How does the Father shape a heart in someone with more compassion for the sick than most? A person who will fast and pray and believe for

---

[11] https://www.ewtn.com/catholicism/library/mother-teresa-the-early-years-2661

strength in someone who is suffering horribly? HaShem allows sores to cover their bodies in Job fashion as they scrape the discharge with broken pottery pieces. Or the Father blinds them for three days like Paul. Adonai gives Paul a thorn in his flesh, Jacob a hip out of socket, and Sarah and Hannah a barren womb. The Father allows a taste of suffering that most cannot imagine. When I first came out of an attack on my health and retired my cane, I sat outside a big meeting one night—a meeting where the megachurch parking lot filled up. Any person coming into the building who was in a wheelchair, using a walker, or a cane, I asked if I could pray for them. I cried with them. I knew what it was like to be sick unto death. I would have never had that compassion if I had not experienced the suffering.

How do you fashion someone to acquire grief for sin that causes them to weep when they see sin? People who have been forgiven much, love much. This love is expressed in uniqueness. A woman's breasts are exposed, and grief occurs in our hearts instead of lust. When we see men and women lusting after fleshpots that we used to partake of, and our hearts do not want to point a finger and yell "repent," but instead, we grab a cloak and cover their nakedness. We cry out as Moses did for his sister, "heal her!" Moses looked at his sister, who had slandered him, and "Moses cried out to the LORD, saying, 'O God, heal her, I pray!'" (Numbers 12:13, NASB).

The Potter's kiln is a place where fire brings forth a vessel worthy of its calling. How do you make a marriage become one in the spirit so that you both think and act and speak the same? Most every night, my husband prays with me—many mornings as well-- but at night he lays his hand on my stomach that refuses to work in divine order due to gastroparesis, and he speaks life over it. He watches it blow up like a balloon, and he sees my tears. With those same tears, he knocks. He asks. He is persistent like the widow who went before the unjust judge, and like Moses, he cries, "Heal my wife!" One night as he prayed, I thought of all the healthy and unhealthy wives who never hear such compassion from their husbands. I thought about how loved I am, how our very marriage has been placed on the Potter's wheel for such a time as this. Every trial, every valley of darkness has brought us closer. For some, it causes bitterness and division. My husband waited twelve years for me. Every year he prayed for a wife and waited. He went on only a few dates because he did not feel they were the ones God had for him. In the twelfth year, a woman at his assembly said, "Jeff, the Father just showed me a field with beautiful flowers, and there the sun was shining down on a blondish brown-haired woman that the Father is 'molding' for you." Eve or Chavah was fashioned and constructed from the side of Adam. The Father was shaping me into a wife for my husband and shaping my husband for me.

So with the Potter sitting at his labor, revolving the wheel with his feet. He is always concerned for his products and turns them out in quantity. With his hands, he molds the clay, and with his feet softens it. His care is for proper coloring, and he keeps watch on the fire of his kiln.

–The Wisdom Books 38:29-30. NAB

To create a piece of pottery, the master potter must form us and fashion us. After the potter forms the clay into the vision he has for it, it is heated at a high temperature in a kiln. This fire of Adonai increases our strength and durability to withstand storms. The Father is shaping you into just the right vessel for His use. It hurts at times to be smashed and remolded into shape, thrown on the wheel, and placed into a fiery pit, but in the end, He will fashion us into a vessel He sees fit to use.

> For You created my innermost parts; You wove me in my mother's womb. I will give thanks to You, because I am awesomely and wonderfully made; Wonderful are Your works, And my soul knows it very well. My frame was not hidden from You When I was made in secret, And skillfully formed in the depths of the earth; Your eyes have seen my formless substance; And in Your book were written All the days that were ordained for me, When as yet there was not one of them.

–Psalms 139:13-16, NASB

There is joy in the suffering when we see the final piece of pottery. May we be filled with a sweet aroma from our spinning on the Potter's wheel. May we take shape and be filled with aww that the Holy One is shaping us into an instrument He can use. "But now, LORD, You are our Father; We are the clay, and You our potter, And all of us are the work of Your hand" (Isaiah 64:8, NASB).

PART 1

Review

1. Do you feel the Potter shaping you? How does molding of clay differ from pruning shears?

2. What resonates with you while meditating on Isaiah 45:9? "Will the pot contend with the Potter or the earthenware with the hand that shapes it? Will the clay ask the Potter what he is making? Or his handiwork say to him, "You have no skill"? (Isaiah 45:9, NEB)

3. Paul was given a thorn in his flesh, Jacob a hip out of socket, and Sarah and Hannah had barren wombs for a season. Have you looked at the Master Potter in this light as One who allows suffering for our greater good?

4. How do great difficulties in our lives draw us closer to our heavenly Father?

5. If Hannah had been given a child at the time of her first request, would she have given the child to the Lord? Would she have had the same amount of joy?

Jumping for Joy In the Midst of Sorrow

PART 2

Speak Life

Sticks and stones may break bones, but words can crush the heart. A word spoken in anger, disgust, and hatred can go deep into our bones and take decades to heal. They are words shot like arrows into our hearts. The root of most of our pain lies hidden deep under the soil. We attempt to keep our pain behind a well-built wall to keep ourselves safe. Many times, the remedy is found by pulling up roots, deep rooted hurts we have suppressed. Excavating ancient relics can at times bring newfound peace and joy.

Recently, I was led to a fantastic article written by Author Ted Hargrove, titled *Seven Things You Should Know About Pain Science*. Hargrove explains how if we feel pain, it is because our brains think our bodies are under some type of threat. Ted uses two examples of trauma where no pain is felt. One, a soldier wounded in battle; two, a shark attack that removes a limb. Ted explains how that person will more than likely feel no pain until the emergency is over. Hargrove goes on to describe something called "allodynia."

> Allodynia is a condition where even normal stimuli such as a light touch to the skin can cause excruciating pain. This is an extreme example of something that might occur quite commonly on a much smaller scale – the nervous system is sensitive to potential threats and sounds the alarm even when no real threat is present. [12]
>
> –Ted Hargrove

A person who has been through trauma, rejection, and stimulation overload could end up in full-blown Allodynia. This condition reminded me of fibromyalgia, a condition I used to suffer from daily which has mostly been healed. Like a car alarm blasting when no one is parked close by, our bodies can have their own alarm going off even when it appears no real threat is present.

I recently became keenly aware of adjectives used to describe pain, whether emotional or physical. What if pain were trying to exhibit something hidden--something more than a title or label diagnosed by a doctor? Could our past tragedies, heartbreak, a bad car wreck, abuse, or fearful experiences be triggered again and felt, with all its excruciating agony, by for example just seeing a car like the one that hit us? Could smelling the same

---

[12] https://www.bettermovement.org/blog/2010/seven-things-you-should-know-about-pain-science

cologne worn by our attacker cause our brain to signal a warning? Could watching a violent movie cause us to re-experience a beating, the trauma, or the same emotions we had as a five-year-old child whose brain sent a signal to run and hide because danger was near? In addition, the body is a complex machine that the original Designer of All Things created. Words that we speak may hold underlying answers about our emotional state, spiritual state, and, yes, physical condition. The first thing I am going to ask you to do is to start listening to your voice. What are some of the things you say when you have any type of pain? Not just the "ouch," I stubbed my toe pain or the lower back pain, but the pain that at times describes our deeper emotions. In an episode in a TV series, a woman severely obese was crying out to lose the weight, but all I heard in my spirit was . . . "Are you carrying a 'heavy load?'" "Is it "weighing" you down or "weighing" on your mind? Do you ever feel weighted down with worry? I am "fed-up!" Think about that term—fed-up. I can barely fit in my clothes.

After a harrowing situation that brought about division in my life, my eyes would not stop weeping for over a month. I began asking the Father what was wrong. No allergy medicine or eye drops seemed to dry up the continuous pouring. One day, I just threw my hands up in the air and said, "Why are my eyes pouring to the point I am carrying a cloth with me everywhere I go to dab them?" Immediately afterward, a friend sent a text message that was a photo shot of Psalms 126. "Those who sow in tears shall harvest with joyful shouting. One who goes here and there weeping, carrying his bag of seed, Shall indeed come again with a shout of joy, bringing his sheaves with him" (Psalms 126:5-6, NASB). Then another friend sent a text with a prayer request for a loved one who had a heart condition causing swelling in her legs and feet and weeping under the skin from much fluid. Sometimes we are weeping inside but cannot express the emotions we are feeling. Any time I have ever done ministry for those shattered and broken, they tend to weep. It doesn't matter if they are grown men tears begin to pour out. This is the first sign of healing. Sometimes the pain in our emotions is so intense it comes out in our skin. Yeshua wept. Yeshua sweated drops of blood. The One who created the universe weeps.

My husband, who suffers from eczema, has to use special soaps, detergents to launder sheets, towels, and clothing. His skin can erupt and become itchy and red. One pharmaceutical company has a new and upcoming drug for this issue, but the commercial explains how eczema can be "under the skin." We like to say things like, "Boy, he or she was really getting under my skin!" Eczema signs and symptoms include tiny blisters that can "weep" and ooze, eventually producing crusted, "thick skin." Hopefully, by now, you are picking up on the use of words here. After so much weeping and oozing, we tend to acquire a thick skin against those who insult us, criticize, or hurt us. We become hardened to difficulties, but our skin can show signs of hidden difficulties. Our inner strengths or weaknesses can be interpreted in organs and health issues. We hear that Jennifer has a weak heart, or possibly our uncle Ken, who died of an enlarged heart. It burst. There is an actual term-- broken heart syndrome.

> For some people, a traumatic event or memory can trigger the physical symptoms of "broken-heart syndrome." Also known as stress-induced cardiomyopathy, takotsubo cardiomyopathy, or apical ballooning syndrome, it's a condition in which heart muscle becomes acutely weak and then fully recovers a few days later.[13]

Another condition, Cancer is a word that comes from the Latin word crab or creeping ulcer. What about diabetes? An old term used for diabetes was called "pissing evil." It comes from a Greek word that means to pass through as urine speedily. The words "diabetes" and "mellitus" have two very separate meanings. They are, however, linked together and have a meaningful connection. Mellitus is pleasant and tasting as honey. Diabetes means passing through as a large discharge of urine. It does not matter what type of diabetes you have; it can lead to excess sugar in the blood. This sugar causes serious health issues. At times, we can "pass through" things quickly with an overly sweet demeanor, but possibly underneath, we are hurting. Are we pissing evil instead of perhaps confronting situations?

---

[13] https://uihc.org/health-topics/ask-expert-what-broken-heart-syndrome

Yes, a spoonful of sugar helps the medicine go down, but a whole pitcher full may be doing more harm than good.

Do we need a chiropractor or massage therapist often? Is your father-in-law or daughter-in-law a "pain in the neck?" Or have they been giving you the "cold shoulder?" What about this one? "My back is tight." Is your back against a wall? Do you feel like you're in a "pinch?" Has someone "hit a nerve?" Take it from someone who was pronounced fully disabled in 2009 at the age of 42; pain in our lives will erupt in our bodies. If we are bruised on the inside, it will flow outward and cause internal conditions. For example, I recently purchased fruit from the store. The fruit was labeled organic and looked yummy on the outside, but it was rotten to the core when I cut it in half. The inside was black. Many times, we have had so much thrown at us and spoken over our souls, we need an eraser. We need a bath or a mikvah to wash off all the phrases enunciated against our amazing temples and all the abuse that has been spoken against us by those in ignorance. How do we find our own identity in the barrage of abuse? There is great joy in knowing our true identity.

If you were raised with parents who suffered from mental issues or low self-esteem, you might have been exposed to this sickness early. Perhaps you heard things like, "He is immature for his age." "Are you eating again?" "She's as skinny as a bean pole." "You will never amount to anything." "Whore—slut." "Bastard." "I never wanted you—I wish you had never been born." "Ugly." The list of words flung through the air like arrows that pierce hearts is without end. We, humans, hurt each other. We judge harshly, and we lack the love of a Father at times. Our broken bodies and hearts need to be injected with the Holy Spirit of Messiah. The collective assembly, the "body," is the community of followers of the Messiah. We are one body. Our bodies are the temple of the Holy Spirit collectively and individually. "And if one member suffers, all the members suffer with it; if one member is honored, all the members rejoice with it" (I Corinthians 12:26, NASB). A King lives inside of us. There is oil in Gilead and healing balm when we seek Him. "Is there no balm in Gilead? Is there no physician there? Why then has not the health of the daughter of my people been restored?" (Jeremiah 8:22, NASB). Picture a clean slate, a feeling many of us felt when we made a covenant with our Father and Yeshua. When we became born anew, we felt like we had been given a bath that removed our past sins and all the words spoken over us. We had baby skin. "Therefore, if anyone is in Christ, he is a new creation. The old has passed away; behold, the new has come" (II Corinthians 5:17, ESV). His Word is said to wash us clean. Instead of soap, picture His Words bathing us, for it surely does.

Have you ever heard someone say something so offensive that when you described what they told you, you used these words? "It went straight through me!" Similar to diarrhea, a word that means "to flow through." The words spoken or the stress of upcoming events is so difficult "to stomach" it just flows through. What about asthma? COPD? Are you finding it hard to breathe in real-time? Do you have to tell yourself to "take a deep breath?" Are the people in your life a breath of fresh air, or are they "suffocating you?" See how that works? Are you continually trying to fill an inner void? An extraordinary verse comes to mind.

> Finally, brothers, whatever is true, whatever is honorable, whatever is just, whatever is pure, whatever is lovely, whatever is commendable, if there is any excellence, if there is anything worthy of praise, think about these things. What you have learned and received and heard and seen in me—practice these things, and the God of peace will be with you.
>
> –Philippians 4:8-9, ESV

We must meditate on things that are pure and lovely. Whether words have anything to do with illnesses, one thing is certain; speaking, life is good medicine. I believe that when we speak powerful words from His Word and we hear them, they can take root in our spirit and cause us to erupt with life. As a plant that is dying, we are nurtured with water and food and words—His Word. We are fearfully and wonderfully made. Let us start using fertilizer and rich soil from His Word that gives life. Let us speak kindly to ourselves, for there is genuine joy in this. "He who believes in Me, as the Scripture said, From his innermost being will flow rivers of living water" (John 7:38, NASB). Our words should flow with living water. Our words should clean, heal, uplift, hold, love, and encompass those who are broken and hurting. A key ingredient to healing our spirit, mind, and body is found in both the Older Testament (Covenant) and New. "And he {Yeshua} said to him, "You shall love the Lord your God with all your heart and with all your soul and with all your mind. This is the great and first commandment. And a second is like it: You shall love your neighbor as yourself" (Matthew 22:37-39, ESV). Today if you find yourself speaking death instead of life, begin to work on your vocabulary. As experienced gardeners, we can start to get to the root of the issues and pull them up. Removing words and damaging language that chokes out the fruit and fresh green life in our lives. Take time to love yourself and know that you are created in the image of the Holy One. Sometimes we must act and seek out a counselor or physician to help us master our vocabulary and heal from past verbal abuse. Whatever it takes, I pray today you begin to be more aware of the words you speak and the power they hold.

PART 2

Review

1. Do you find it easier to speak words filled with life over others but not yourself?

2. How do words from youth still affect us today?

3. According to Yeshua's words in Luke 6, can we connect loving ourselves to speaking differently about who we are in Him? "The good person out of the good treasure of his heart brings forth what is good; and the evil person out of the evil treasure brings forth what is evil; for his mouth speaks from that which fills his heart" (Luke 6:45, NASB).

4. How careful are we with our words with and about others?

5. Yeshua is the living Word. How can meditating on His Words change our words? Give an example.

PART 3

Light Birthed in Darkness

Beethoven was born December 17, 1770. His date of birth fell on the 7th day of Chanukah (Hanukkah) in the Hebrew month of Kislev. In John Chapter 10, we read about Yeshua keeping this Festival of Lights. Although Hanukkah always begins on the 25th day of Kislev, that date can fall anywhere between late November and late December on the Gregorian calendar. Beethoven's birth, name, and deafness all orchestrate a melody. And just like the celebration of Hanukkah, Beethoven shone his light in the darkness. Though he became deaf, his spirit man could hear music inside his soul. "The name Kislev derives from the Hebrew word *kesel* (כֶּסֶל). In Hebrew, the word for kidney is also *kesel* (כֶּסֶל)." [14]

Hearing the most profound truth is attributed to the kidneys. A kidney sliced in half looks like ears. "You are near in their mouth but far from their kidneys" (Jeremiah 12:2 ISR).

---

[14] https://www.inner.org/times/kislev/kislev.htm

Bible translators have replaced the word *kidney* with *rein* or *heart* and often as *inward parts*, but kidneys was the original wording. Beethoven's autopsy report showed he had renal disease among a whole list of health issues. A man who lost his hearing gave us music orchestrated in heavenly silence that could only be heard in Beethoven's mind.

Ludwig van Beethoven is a name familiar to most people over the globe. He wrote nine symphonies that took music to another galaxy. But it is his personal life and calling that is most noteworthy. This man suffered horribly, and, yet, his heart-wrenching soul was able to strike keys and soar violin bows into a place of melodies leaving one mesmerized. I often say our pain is for another man's gain. Frequently the world sees the gift and not the person. We know Beethoven because of his masterpieces. I can listen to *Fur Elise* or *Beethoven 9th Symphony – Movement IV – "Ode to Joy"* daily, but what about the man who composed them?

Beethoven's name from birth seems profoundly chosen. *Van* meaning from and Beethoven meaning gardens or fields. *Ludwig*, Beethoven's first name, has many metaphors connected to his journey. The first element means *famed* and *loud*, from Proto-Indo-European t*o hear*. The second element is *wīg*, meaning *battle* or *strife*. A man who battled hearing loss with great strife would become loud and famous for his musical brilliance. Yes, his name has all those facets embedded in it. [15]

Kislev is the 9th month of the Hebrew calendar. It represents the time of pregnancy in the womb. Kislev expresses that all life is precious. Beethoven's mother lost two sons before giving birth to Beethoven, one of them being her first husband's; however, she lost even more children. Besides her sons Beethoven, Caspar, and Johann, she had three more children (one boy and two girls). All of them died soon in life, respectively at the age of four days, one year, and two years. She is poetically described by Edmund Morris.

> Her final confinement left her depressed and frail, doomed to expire herself, at forty, of consumption. Slender, earnest-eyed, moralistic, genteel, she floats like a faded watercolor sketch in the van Beethoven family scrapbook, amid more robust images of men of high color and stocky build.
>
> –Edmund Morris

Beethoven's father, Johann, was a drunk and a mediocre court singer. He sang in the chapel of the Archbishop of Cologne in Bonn. However, Beethoven looked up to his grandfather, whom he was named after -- Kapellmeister (Master) Ludwig van Beethoven, Bonn's most affluent and celebrated musician. His

---
[15] https://www.behindthename.com/name/ludwig

home was filled with silver and wealth, while Beethoven's father's house was filled with banknotes and poverty. Beethoven's father taught him music. According to Biography:

> Sometime between the births of his two younger brothers, Beethoven's father began teaching him music with extraordinary rigor and brutality that affected him for the rest of his life. Neighbors provided accounts of the small boy weeping while he played the clavier, standing atop a footstool to reach the keys, his father beating him for each hesitation or mistake. [16]
>
> –Biography

The one area that brought Beethoven much pain would also bring him fame and joy. Many times our gifting can cause us pain and joy. Beethoven was deprived of sleep for extra hours of practice. On a near-daily basis, he was flogged and locked in the cellar by his father, but one cannot hide light in the darkness because a lamp will only shine brighter. "He [Beethoven] studied the violin and clavier with his father as well as taking additional lessons from organists around town. Whether in spite of or because of his father's draconian methods, Beethoven was a prodigiously talented musician from his earliest days." Biography. [17] Sadly, later in life, Beethoven received custody of his nephew and was often cruel like his father had been to him.

---

[16] Ludwig van Beethoven - Symphonies, Deafness & Race - Biography
[17] Ludwig van Beethoven - Symphonies, Deafness & Race - Biography

We often do what we know until we know better. Beethoven longed for his nephew to be a musician, but the young man was not gifted in this area.

By the age of 13, some historians say, Beethoven became Assistant Court Musician and was placed on salary to support his family because his father's alcoholism had reached the point that he could no longer provide for the family. In 1787, the court sent Beethoven to Vienna, where he longed to study with Mozart. "Tradition has it that, upon hearing Beethoven, Mozart said, "Keep your eyes on him; someday he will give the world something to talk about." [18] Some historians, however, are skeptical that Mozart and Beethoven met at all. While it cannot be determined whether Beethoven met Mozart, it is feasible that Beethoven heard Mozart play. When the Father sends people who want to learn or be mentored by us, we should mimic this story. Although Beethoven had a cruel upbringing, many later compositions much were for the sole purpose of exalting the Father of Lights and more so after losing his hearing.

Beethoven started becoming deaf at around the age of 26. The intense buzzing in his ears caused irritability, and for many years, the people around him had no idea he was suffering. As a writer, I cannot imagine losing my eyesight. I never know what story will come forth from my fingers until I start writing. Beethoven's ears were on straining to hear a vibration. While

---
[18] Ludwig van Beethoven - Symphonies, Deafness & Race - Biography

giving piano instructions to a Hungarian countess, Beethoven fell in love with her, but he could not marry her because of his social status. He later dedicated his *Moonlight" Sonata No. 14* to her. He wrote, "No friend have I. I must live by myself alone, but I know well that God is nearer to me than others in my art, so I will walk fearlessly with Him." [19]

Not only was Beethoven's social status against him, but his appearance was also rather unique. Beethoven's ruddy complexion bore the scars of childhood smallpox. His unruly dark hair and bushy eyebrows stood out, making his sorrowful eyes only more dramatized. His deafness was socially awkward for him. He was a short man and unprofessional in his behavior. I am reminded of a passage that may have comforted Beethoven. It is a passage written concerning the Messiah. "He had no stately form or majesty that we should look upon Him, Nor appearance that we should be attracted to Him." (Isaiah 53:2). German composer, Ferdinand Ries, a pupil, friend, and secretary to Beethoven, described Beethoven in words one would never have guessed while listening to his musical masterpieces.

> His clumsy movements lacked all grace. He rarely picked up anything without dropping or breaking it. Everything was knocked over, soiled, or destroyed. How he ever

---

[19] https://selfeducatedamerican.com/2015/12/17/ludwig-van-beethovens-faith-in-god/

managed to shake himself at all remains difficult to understand, even considering the frequent cuts on his cheeks. – He never learned to dance in time with the music. [20]

–Ferdinand Ries

A man so highly gifted in one area yet lacking in so many others. Listening to *Moon Light Sonata #14* does not evoke an image of a dyslexic, clumsy, awkward man with no rhythm. Many times when a person is gifted in one area, and that area is sensitively magnified, he may be quite challenged in other areas. Several close friends left a multitude of adjectives to describe this creative genius. Beethoven's personality was also challenging.

As a young man, Beethoven was frank to the point of rudeness. Headstrong and proud, he was never willing to conform in his behavior. As he grew older and deafness overtook him, the negative aspects of Beethoven's personality came to the fore. He was increasingly given to bouts of despair, the difficulties of communication made him more reserved, and he became more suspicious and distrustful of others. [21]

–Barry Cooper, ed The Beethoven Companion (London, 1991), 102 - 105

---

[20] http://toddtarantino.com/hum/beethovenhimself.html
[21] https://www.jstor.org/stable/736210?seq=1

Hearing and seeing are vital in the spiritual sense. All of Beethoven's talents, creativity, frankness,

headstrong, and opinionated spirit would be humbled through deafness. His deafness caused suffering. Beethoven now lacked the ability to hear and respond with great authority or pomp. Many of these difficulties led Beethoven to seek a heavenly Father but multiple writings paint this man to be utterly unpredictable. Domestic luxuries were unimportant to him, and the careful composer was a creature of disorderliness. Baron de Tremont writes of a visit to Beethoven in 1809.

> Picture to yourself the dirtiest, most disorderly place imaginable – blotches of moisture covered the ceiling, an oldish grand piano, on which dust disputed the place with various pieces of engraved and manuscript music; under the piano (I do not exaggerate) an unemptied pot de nuit; (portable toilet) the chairs, mostly cane-seated, were covered with plates bearing the remains of last night's supper and with wearing apparel, etc.
>
> –Barry Cooper, ed The Beethoven Companion (London, 1991), 102 - 105

Count von Keglevics, the nephew of one of Beethoven's students, wrote:

> He had a whim, one of many, since he lived across from her [his student], of coming to give her lessons clad in a dressing gown, slippers, and a peaked nightcap.

Many times, those gifted with extreme wealth in one area are labeled strange in another. Beethoven could not spell very well or do simple math, but he could indeed compose. Because Beethoven dropped out of traditional school at 10, he never learned the fundamentals. Multiple historians believe he had learning disabilities and possibly dyslexia. From reading the few comments left by acquaintances and knowledge of his upbringing, it is easy to see the genius was still suffering from trauma, suspicions, and a fear of a world where people often did not understand him. Beethoven was most comfortable alone in his apartment wearing pajamas and writing music in his head from the memory of what each musical note held. Bathing was overrated and cleaning up would take away from the very thing that had been beaten into him from childhood.

In his earlier days, Beethoven would leave Bonn and travel abroad, teaching students and being taught by the likes of Hayden and other greats. It has been said that this free-spirited man, Beethoven, rewrote the rule book for Classical music. Robert Greenberg, Ph.D., music historian and faculty member at the University of Pennsylvania's Wharton School of Business, share multiple layers of knowledge concerning Beethoven in a blog by Harvard Business titled *In a Crisis, What Would Beethoven Do? Rewrite the Rulebook.*

"Beethoven bent, folded, spindled, and mutilated the Classical style, believing completely that its rules, rituals, and traditions were only useful up to the point that they served the expressive context. Beyond that, he reserved the right to do exactly what he pleased."

Greenberg continued describing details of this man's life through anger and sickness and the moment when Beethoven went completely deaf.

> Unlike most alienated and isolated people, Beethoven translated his experience into action, not by writing sour letters to the editor or by yelling at the neighbor's kids, but by composing music that universalized both his problems and solutions. His problems are well known; his solutions, always, grew out of an instinct and ability to rewrite the rulebook when environmental and personal issues threatened to crush him. [9]
>
> –Robert Greenberg

In his later years, reaching total deafness, Beethoven depended on writing pads or notebooks to communicate. He stayed isolated in his apartment much of the time. Many of these conversations written on notepads have survived. Some of them are only one-sided, but they give the reader much to ponder. On one occasion, it seems Beethoven was discussing the Resurrection with his friend Karl Peters. We don't know what question Beethoven asked, but Peters' reply sums up the contemporary crisis of faith and the hope of overcoming it: "You will arise with me from the dead—because you must. Religion remains constant, and only Man is changeable." [22] Taking advice from one physician, during his darkest days of depression, Beethoven took to nature.

> My miserable hearing does not trouble me here. In the country, it seems as if every tree said to me: 'Holy! Holy!' Who can give complete expression to the ecstasy of the woods! O, the sweet stillness of the woods! July 1814
>
> –Ludwig van Beethoven

Also in 1814, in a rehearsal for the Archduke Trio, it was said that Beethoven pounded on the keys until the strings jangled, and in piano, he played so softly that whole groups of notes were absent. His deafness had crippled his ability to discern this. How many of us have a beautiful melody inside, but at times, when we try to orchestrate the words, they come out harsh?

> When it came to the premiere of his massive Ninth Symphony, Beethoven insisted on conducting. The orchestra hired another conductor, Michael Umlauf, to stand alongside the composer. Umlauf told the performers to follow him and ignore Beethoven's directions. The symphony received rapturous applause, which Beethoven could not hear. Legend has it that the young contralto Carolina Unger approached the maestro

---

[22] Beethoven and the Catholic Church (crisismagazine.com)

and turned him around to face the audience, to see the ovation.

–The Project Gutenberg eBook of The Life of Ludwig van Beethoven, Volume III (of 3), by Alexander Wheelock Thayer.

We, too, are often conducting our own symphony. Many times, the Father is present orchestrating each movement. Other times we are doing things to be seen by men. "So, when you give to the poor, do not sound a trumpet before you, as the hypocrites do in the synagogues and in the streets, so that they may be honored by men. Truly I say to you, they have their reward in full" (Matthew 6:2, NASB). Sometimes we just need help with the gift.

One day, we too pray that Yeshua will turn us toward the Father, and we will hear, "Well done my good and faithful servant." In the meantime, let us become so swept up in Him that we do not even hear the accolades of men. Our gift is for the Father. We work with our hands to glorify Him. Can we be so caught up in His Glory that even our weaknesses become our strengths? Paul said, "Therefore I delight in weaknesses, in insults, in distresses, in persecutions, in difficulties, in behalf of Christ; for when I am weak, then I am strong" (II Corinthians 12:10, NASB).

We are often surrounded by dirty chamber pots, needing a change of garments or warmth, pounding on keys to make a melody for Adonai that we often cannot even hear, and yet, the Father is mindful of us. May we run the race with horse blinders on, running to get the prize, even with our imperfections and times of deafness. Not a prize given to men by men, but a prize that transcends time. In Beethoven's later years, he produced some of his most admired work, and he was utterly deaf at that time. When we have spiritual ears, we can still hear the melody of heaven. Our outward bodies are perishing daily, but our spirit man grows stronger. I laughed at the last words recorded by Beethoven, "Pity, pity—too late!" as the dying composer was told of a gift of twelve bottles of wine from his publisher.

Beethoven's father wanted his son to become Mozart. As a piano virtuoso, Beethoven grew to surpass Mozart in measures unheard of. Every flower has its day in the sun when its colors burst forth, and people walk by and say, "Look at the beauty of those orchids, roses, and daffodils and smell their sweet aroma." But once the colors fade and the petals drop, the stems bend, shrinking towards the earth, that season is over. May we all work while it is still light and let us shine even in the darkest cellar. What can we learn from this man who was physically deaf, yet brilliantly hearing melodies full of wonder? Is there joy hidden in sorrow? Is there sound hidden in silence. Are there melodies in our hearts that long to sing even if no one hears our voice but heaven? What type of strength can we learn from these dealt cards that could not be discarded at a round table? Can you see the music and melody of suffering and sorrow sitting right next to those piano keys of joy?

Some sources have listed his last words as, "I shall hear in heaven." And so shall we, friends. During the month of Kislev, the month of dreams, the month of light in the darkness may we dream, and may we get to the very root of the riddle. May we hear and obey. May we take our precious gifts from Abba and use them as Beethoven did. Even with the loss of his natural hearing, he could still hear the music. Even with our disfigurement, our frailties, our lack of communication skills, our dyslexia, our past beatings, and cruelties, may we shine.

PART 3

Review

1. What does your birth name mean? Who were you named after?

2. What joyful thoughts come to mind reading this quote by Beethoven? "My miserable hearing does not trouble me here. In the country, it seems as if every tree said to me: 'Holy! Holy!'

3. Have you ever listened to Ode to Joy? If so, did you enjoy it?

4. How does our upbringing affect our future?

5. Can you think of others with disabilities like Beethoven, that despite their deafness, blindness, paralysis, etc., used their life and gifts to help and inspire others?

Jumping for Joy In the Midst of Sorrow

SECTION # 6

Darkness and Light

The next three devotionals gets to the deepest heart of the matter concerning sorrow, and the end of sorrows completed work.

> *I form the light and create the darkness; I bring prosperity and create calamity. I, the LORD, do all these things.*
>
> *– Isaiah 45:7, BSB*

Jumping for Joy In the Midst of Sorrow

PART 1

David Danced

The God of Abraham, Isaac, and Jacob instructed Moses to make a tabernacle on earth that was a replica of the tabernacle in heaven. Adonai gives Moses instructions and warnings to not differentiate from His blueprint. Two cherubim (*Keruvim* in Hebrew) guard the Mercy Seat above the Ark of the Covenant. Two angels with flaming swords guard the Tree of Life. The Ark is the heart of the sanctuary--the very place where the Word of Adonai dwells. The Ark of the Covenant (*Aron*, in Hebrew) means chest. Our chest area holds our heart. We are told to hide Adonai's Word in our heart, so we do not sin against Him. Three items resided in this chest, the tablet with the Ten Commandments or Ten Sayings, Aaron's rod that budded, and the heavenly manna.

> Behind the second veil there was a tabernacle which is called the Most Holy Place, having a golden altar of incense and the ark of the covenant covered on all sides with gold, in which was a golden jar holding the manna,

> Aaron's staff which budded, and the tablets of the covenant; and above it were the cherubim of glory overshadowing the atoning cover; but about these things we cannot now speak in detail.
>
> –Hebrews 9:3-5, NASB

In II Samuel, the Ark of the Covenant had been captured by the Philistines. Now, David, the new king, is ready to bring this precious vessel to Jerusalem. Can you imagine the joy and anticipation of David's heart as this king is preparing for such holy furniture? I am sure David envisioned this journey with splendor and triumph, but, unfortunately, during the transitioning of the Ark, death occurred. These situations happen in our lives too. Death is residing right next to life. Sorrow is sitting right next to joy. As David and all the House of Israel were rejoicing before the Father, making music with lyres, harps, tambourines, and cymbals, something went wrong. In a matter of seconds, one man's hand reaches to steady this box made of the same wood used to create a crown of thorns on our Messiah's head, and the man is struck dead. His name is Uzzah. The Ark overlaid in pure gold was not an empty vessel. Uzzah's hand was not touching an empty box. Spiritually, the Ark was the manifestation of God's physical presence on earth, His Holy Breath--Wind. When the Father spoke with Moses in the Tent of Meeting, He did so from between the two *keruvim*. This man,

Uzzah, who reaches to steady the chest from falling, is struck in an instant. Death, anger, and a holy fear fill the people.

Interestingly, Shiloh was the home of the tabernacle for 369 years. When the Philistines captured the Ark, they were pressed to bring it back because outbreaks of tumors and disease afflicted them. Their fish god, Dagon, lay crumpled, decapitated, with his hands broken off in front of the Ark. Again, this was no ordinary piece of furniture. Then the people sent a message to Kiriath-jearim to come and get the Ark, which they did until David arrived.

> Now He fatally struck some of the men of Beth-shemesh because they had looked into the ark of the LORD. He struck 50,070 men among the people, and the people mourned because the LORD had struck the people with a great slaughter. And the men of Beth-shemesh said, "Who is able to stand before the LORD, this holy God? And to whom will He go up from us?" So they sent messengers to the inhabitants of Kiriath-jearim, saying, "The Philistines have brought back the ark of the LORD; come down and take it up to yourselves."
>
> –I Samuel 6:19-21, NASB

From Ashdod to Gath to Ekron, the Ark brought destruction. The people of these territories cried out to send away the Ark of the God of Israel, for tumors came upon them and many died. This story is reminiscent of Aaron's sons, Nadab and Abihu, who took their respective firepans and placed incense on them. They offered what the Bible calls "strange fire" before Adonai. This was a fire God had not commanded them to bring. This fire consumed their bodies. They were carried outside the camp. Exodus 25 and 26 give warning that they were not to differentiate from the pattern shown. Aaron's sons lay dead in their priestly garments, but their dead bodies could not stay in a place that represented life, so they were carried outside the holy place. Hebrews 8:5 explains that the earthly tabernacle with all its articles serves as a copy and shadow of what is in the heavens. The heavens declare the Glory of Adonai—they are always obedient, but sadly, Aaron's sons were not, and neither was David.

> But when they came to the threshing floor of Nacon, Uzzah reached out toward the ark of God and took hold of it, because the oxen nearly overturned it. And the anger of the LORD burned against Uzzah, and God struck him down there for his irreverence; and he died there by the ark of God. Then David became angry because of the LORD'S outburst against Uzzah; and that place has been called Perez-uzzah to this day.
>
> —II Samuel 6:6-8, NASB

According to Abarim Publications, "The word Nachon means smitten, stricken, and it has been determined." The oxen had shaken Adonai's most Holy Place where His Spirit resided. The

Word, the Holy Ones' Seed, lived inside of that Ark overlaid in pure gold. In a similar story, Judah's son Onan wasted his seed and spilled it on the ground. He, too, is struck dead.

> Onan knew that the offspring would not be his; so when he went in to his brother's wife, he wasted his seed on the ground in order not to give offspring to his brother.
>
> −Genesis 38:9, NASB

In the Book of Acts, a married couple is struck dead for lying to the Holy Spirit concerning land they sold.

> But Peter said, "Ananias, why has Satan filled your heart to lie to the Holy Spirit and to keep back some of the proceeds of the land? While it remained unsold, did it not remain your own? And after it was sold, was it not under your control? Why is it that you have conceived this deed in your heart? You have not lied to men, but to God." And as he heard these words, Ananias collapsed and died; and great fear came over all who heard about it. The young men got up and covered him up, and after carrying him out, they buried him.
>
> −Acts 5:3-6, NASB

Ananias's wife, Sapphira, is stuck dead too for lying to the Holy Spirit. The Ark David was carrying held this Holy Spirit. Uzzah was reacting to the Ark falling, and he was trying to steady it, but David had taken short-cuts. The king was in a hurry with Holy things? In I Chronicles, we learn that David was not being obedient to the instructions for carrying the Ark, the Most Holy Place. They were carrying it on a cart with oxen the first time. It is then, after the death of Uzzah, that the Ark goes to rest for three months in the house of Obed-Edom.

> David was afraid of God that day, saying, "How can I bring the ark of God home to me?" So David did not take the Ark with him to the city of David, but took it aside to the house of Obed-edom the Gittite. Thus the Ark of God remained with the family of Obed-edom in his house three months; and the LORD blessed the family of Obed-edom with all that he had.
>
> –I Chronicles 13:12-14, NASB

David had a holy fear of Adonai that day. Obed-edom was not fearful of taking the Ark even though a man died by touching it. Obed had reverence. We carry His Spirit in our temples and often do not have a holy fear or awe of what that means. David eventually takes the Ark to its resting place, but he does what is right this time. David follows the pattern and instructions given to Moses from God on how to carry this golden box.

> Now David built houses for himself in the city of David; and he prepared a place for the Ark of God and pitched a tent for it. Then David said, "No one is to carry the ark of God but the Levites; for the LORD chose them to carry the

ark of God and to minister to Him forever.

—I Chronicles 15:1-2, NASB

Could our sorrow at times come because we are not carrying holy things properly? David admits that they did not carry the Ark as Moses had commanded. No one was to carry the Ark but the Levites. Because of these circumstances, death happened. The death occurred during what should have been life and joy.

> Then David called for the priests Zadok and Abiathar, and for the Levites, for Uriel, Asaiah, Joel, Shemaiah, Eliel, and Amminadab; and he said to them, "You are the heads of the fathers' households of the Levites; consecrate yourselves, you and your relatives, so that you may bring up the ark of the LORD God of Israel to the place that I have prepared for it. Because you did not carry it at the first, the LORD our God made an outburst against us, since we did not seek Him according to the ordinance.

—I Chronicles 15:11-13, NASB

David now dances before the Ark, and he does something else that possibly he would not have done if the horrible death of Uzzah had not happened. King David appoints the Levites as ministers before the Ark. He appoints musicians to play music before the Ark, and one of them is Obed-Edom. This man shows honor to the Most Holy Chest. On top of that, David had several blow trumpets before the Ark of the Covenant, continually. Worship in David's tent ends with thanksgiving, and the song is recorded in I Chronicles 16. The song is filled with joy and praise. Read each stanza and picture the whole earth full of His Glory and His everlasting joy. Sometimes calamity happens because we are not carrying His Spirit correctly like David when he moved the Ark. Sometimes, we take for granted that we are to be lamps illuminated by the Son.

Oh, give thanks to the LORD, call upon His name;
> Make known His deeds among the peoples.

Sing to Him, sing praises to Him;
> Speak of all His wonders.

Glory in His holy name;
> Let the heart of those who seek the LORD be glad.

Seek the LORD and His strength;
> Seek His face continually.

Remember His wonderful deeds which He has done,
> His marvels and the judgments from His mouth,

O seed of Israel His servant,
> Sons of Jacob, His chosen ones!

He is the LORD our God;
> His judgments are in all the earth.

Remember His covenant forever,
> The word which He commanded to a thousand generations,

The covenant which He made with Abraham,
    And His oath to Isaac.

He also confirmed it to Jacob for a statute,
    To Israel as an everlasting covenant,

Saying, "To you, I will give the land of Canaan,
    As the portion of your inheritance."

When they were only a few in number,
    Very few, and strangers in it,

And they wandered about from nation to nation,
    And from one kingdom to another people,

He permitted no man to oppress them,
    And He reproved kings for their sakes, saying,

"Do not touch My anointed ones,
    And do My prophets no harm."

Sing to the LORD, all the earth;
    Proclaim good tidings of His salvation from day today.

Tell of His glory among the nations,
    His wonderful deeds among all the peoples.

For great is the LORD, and greatly to be praised;
    He also is to be feared above all gods.

For all the gods of the peoples are idols,
> But the LORD made the heavens.

Splendor and majesty are before Him,
> Strength and joy are in His place.

Ascribe to the LORD, O families of the peoples,
> Ascribe to the LORD glory and strength.

Ascribe to the LORD the glory due His name;
> Bring an offering, and come before Him;
> Worship the LORD in holy array.

Tremble before Him, all the earth;
> Indeed, the world is firmly established, it will not be moved.

Let the heavens be glad, and let the earth rejoice;
> And let them say among the nations, "The LORD reigns."

Let the sea roar, and all it contains;
> Let the field exult, and all that is in it.

Then the trees of the forest will sing for joy before the LORD;
> For He is coming to judge the earth.

O give thanks to the LORD, for He is good;
> For His lovingkindness is everlasting.

Then say, "Save us, O God of our salvation,

And gather us and deliver us from the nations,
To give thanks to Your holy name,
And glory in Your praise."

Blessed be the LORD, the God of Israel,
From everlasting even to everlasting.
Then all the people said, "Amen," and praised the LORD.

–I Chronicles 16:8-36, NASB

PART 1

Review

1. Have you ever experienced joy and sorrow simultaneously?

2. Psalm 100 tells us to enter His gates with thanksgiving, and His courtyards with praise. How often do we try to rush in quickly like David with the Ark?

3. Sometimes tragic events happen that cause us to fear the Holy One in greater measure. Can you think of a time when something unforeseen occurred that made you change how you felt about Adonai?

4. After the death of Uzzah, David moves the Ark according to the instructions the Lord laid out. David then dances before the Ark. What pictures fill your mind as you envision this glorious day?

5. Uzzah's error cost him his life. How does his story change your thoughts towards Adonai and His instructions He has laid out for us in His Torah?

PART 2

Who has a Broken Heart?

One morning in 2010, I peered into the reflection of the mirror, and I wondered who the person was staring back at me. I had been too depleted financially to get my hair done at a beauty shop and was taken by a friend to a hair design school. This is a shop where the students are learning to cut hair. They practice their training on brave individuals looking for cheaper pricing. I sat nervously in the chair as the dye was placed on my head and the foils. Soon I was ushered under the dryer, but something kept running down my neck. The hair dye had seeped through the foil. After shampooing, the stylist showed me the brown spots that had run, bled, and dried. There were large dark brown spots in my blonde hair that looked horrible. Her assistant came out, the manager, and soon a host of women were standing around my chair trying to decide what to do with the mess, and it was a mess. The manager asked if she could re-dye and cut my hair. I nodded and sat in shock as I heard her clippers begin to shave the back of my head in a boy-type haircut that left me with about an inch or two of hair on top that she spiked with gel. The color of red dye she chose for me was more of a burgundy and covered the dark brown spots. It was such a drastically different look that I still had trouble gazing into the mirror when it was time to go out in public.

Losing my hair was just an outward sign. I lost so many things I loved with such swiftness that it seemed like one blow would knock me to my knees, and before I could recover from the next one, down I would go again. The pain I felt seemed to seep out of my pores. I felt as if I were walking around with blood oozing from my heart. I kept dabbing at the seeping place of my heart, applying pressure, but to no avail. This pain was so heavy it made breathing problematic. I drove the short distance to the church assembly and made my way inside with my new fashion statements -- my cane and red hair. Just trying to stand during one song was a struggle for me. Although I was better and able to drive some, I was still exhausted from chronic fatigue and other neurological issues. Losing my health was more like losing my freedom.

Everything that identified me as a person was plucked away. I began to talk to Job as if he and I were old friends. I asked, Job what did it feel like when the messenger came with the news of more pain? How did you bow and begin to worship our Lord after hearing of the death of your children, your livestock, your servants, your health? I sighed and hobbled out of the mini-van and entered the sanctuary. I tried to focus on the people around me in the pews. They smiled, clapped their hands, and sang loudly. Many had joy that I coveted. Genuine joy. I am sure they all had a story of their own sorrow and losses. It seemed many I encountered did.

The pastor's message was well needed, and many scriptures he quoted seem to speak to me, encourage me even. He was gifted in the prophetic and humble, and I knew I was where I was supposed to be going then. I had just started driving this short distance to fellowship with other believers a few months prior, but sitting alone on the pew was just a reminder that everything in my life had become empty.

I knew the Lord had taken the desire from my eyes in more ways than one when he took my husband, the man I had shared my life with. The Lord was in control, but the pain was unbearable some days. I missed people. I missed my pets, stepdaughter, job, life as I knew it, and, yes, a man who left me. My children were living on their own or with others due to my situation. I could not help but wonder how the Father could take my life and make anything out of it again. It seemed hopeless. I was too sick to start over and too empty. I did not know then that God loved empty vessels that He could fill. Elijah said to the empty widow, "Go outside, borrow vessels from all your neighbors, empty vessels and not too few" (II Kings 4:2, ESV). The widow borrowed, and the oil poured forth and filled them all. Possibly, I needed to become empty so He could pour in His oil and His Spirit and do something new in my life.

The service was coming to a close, and soon the minister asked if there was anyone who needed healing in their body. He quoted a verse from the book of James.

> Is anyone among you sick? Let him call for the elders of the church, and let them pray over him, anointing him with oil in the name of the Lord. And the prayer of faith will save the one who is sick, and the Lord will raise him up.
>
> –James 5:14-25, ESV

I stood there on wobbly legs, my cane in hand, but did not budge from my seat. I watched as many made their way down to the altar. I listened as the minister placed his hands on the heads of the many and began to pray for each one. My heart hurt. At that moment, I began to notice the seeping of sorrow and the constant throbbing that seemed to take my very breath. My heart felt like a sieve that blood was pouring out of. Help. I began to scream inside my soul, pleading even, "Oh Lord, I am sick in my body, this is true, but my heart is broken in a million pieces. Please heal my heart. Lord, can you take this grief away? It is more than I can endure." I began to cry and ask Him over and over until something profound happened. Something so incredibly intimate it brought tears that poured down my face like constant rain. Suddenly the minister raised the microphone to his lips and said, "I need everyone to stop for a minute. I need your attention. The Lord is telling me that there is a person here who has a broken heart, and I can see it. It's battered, shredded, and bruised. Where are you?" He began to look over the congregation, and I raised my hand--my small insignificant hand. He said, people, I want you all to lay hands on our sister as we pray for the Father to heal her heart. In that precious moment, I suddenly didn't care about my heart. I was so in awe that the Father of glory heard me and that He loved me enough to speak to His minister that I was awestruck. The Lord loved me enough to stop praying over people with physical ailments to envelop me and let me know He knew. He saw. He wanted to take His Son's nail-scarred hands and hold my gaping places, pat the blood that had oozed out and cover it with His healing blood. Oh, I needed a Savior in more ways than one and one that was intricate and detailed. The Father spoke in a whisper that blew across my heart and held it to His. Oh, what a glorious Savior we serve, and He does not show partiality. "Then Peter began to speak: "I now truly understand that God does not show favoritism" (Acts 10:34, BSB).

If you need healing from a broken heart, the Father wants to minister to you today. He sees your tears. He desires for you to be made whole spiritually, physically, and mentally. Raise your hands to the heavens and picture His loving arms enveloping you. "He heals the brokenhearted And binds up their wounds" (Psalm 147:3, NASB).

PART 2

Review

1. How does our outer appearance at times affect our inward self? Can you think of a time when you drastically changed your appearance, whether by losing or gaining weight, hair loss, or a new hairstyle that caused you to change inwardly?

2. How does internally healing from pain, loss, and bitterness affect our health?

3. When the minister stopped the prayer service and spoke the words about someone needing the heart healed, I was in complete shock. Can you think of a time in your life when the Father shocked or surprised you?

4. How many different ways does the Lord speak to you?

5. In Luke 18, Yeshua tells a parable about a persistent widow. What can we learn from this story and not wavering during times of great sorrow?

Then Jesus told them a parable about their need to pray at all times and not lose heart: "In a certain town there was a judge who neither feared God nor respected men. And there was a widow in that town who kept appealing to him, 'Give me justice against my adversary.' For a while he refused, but later he said to himself, 'Though I neither fear God nor respect men, yet because this widow keeps pestering me, I will give her justice. Then she will stop wearing me out with her perpetual requests.'" And the Lord said, "Listen to the words of the unjust judge. Will not God bring about justice for His elect who cry out to Him day and night? Will He continue to defer their help? I tell you, He will promptly carry out justice on their behalf. Nevertheless, when the Son of Man comes, will He find faith on earth?"
–Luke 18:1-8, BSB

Jumping for Joy In the Midst of Sorrow

PART 3

Joy and Barrenness

The mighty prophet Elijah arrives at a widow's house, and she is gathering sticks to make a fire. The prophet requests a jar of water and a piece of bread, but the widow remarks that she has no bread, only a handful of flour in a bowl and a little oil in a jar. The widow tells Elijah that she is gathering a few sticks to prepare the last meal for her and her son. They were ready to eat this last supper and then die because the famine was so severe. The prophet has already been told that the Father of glory has prepared a widow to provide for him. He does not question how this can happen with a smidgeon of oil and a handful of flour. Elijah knows the Father is not a man that He should lie to him and not provide. Our Father can bring water out of a rock and rain down bread from heaven. He parts the sea and causes the dead to rise. He shuts the mouths of hungry lions and opens prison doors. Elijah knows His Power.

Elijah said to her,

Do not fear; go, do as you have said, but make me a little bread cake from it first and bring it out to me, and afterward, you may make one for yourself and for your son. "For thus says the LORD God of Israel, 'The bowl of flour shall not be exhausted, nor shall the jar of oil be empty, until the day that the LORD sends rain on the face of the earth.'"

–I Kings 17:13-14, NASB

What a miraculous testimony. Every day the widow had faith that Adonai would supply bread and oil, but sometimes it seems as if the Father shows favor and pours blessings on everyone but us. We watch as they give birth to dream after dream while we stay barren. We watch as, one by one, their prayers are answered. Meanwhile, our prayers feel as if they cannot get airborne. Our petitions go unanswered. No one even lays hands on our dead, dried-up wombs. But is there a reason for this season? Is there a greater work happening inside our souls? Could He be birthing something in us that needs to be birthed slowly and seasoned over time? Are we often trusting in our own strength and not waiting for patience to do its complete work? "Consider it all joy, my brothers and sisters, when you encounter various trials, knowing that the testing of your faith produces endurance. And let endurance have its perfect result, so that you may be perfect and complete, lacking in nothing" (James 1:2-3, NASB).

The story of Samuel's birth has always been dear to my heart, so much so that I named my youngest son after the great, mighty prophet. But it was his mother's sacrifice that touched my soul. A man named Elkanah had two wives, one named Hannah and the other named Peninnah. Peninnah bore children, but Hannah was barren and bore none. Elkanah went out of his city yearly to sacrifice to the Lord and worship in the town of Shiloh.

> When the day came that Elkanah sacrificed, he would give portions to his wife Peninnah and to all her sons and daughters; but to Hannah he would give a double portion, because he loved Hannah, but the LORD had closed her womb. Her rival, moreover, would provoke her bitterly to irritate her, because the LORD had closed her womb. And it happened year after year, as often as she went up to the house of the LORD, that she would provoke her; so she wept and would not eat.
>
> –I Samuel 14:5-7, NASB

The Father had shut Hannah's womb for a season and a reason. He works in mysterious ways, but there is always a purpose behind the barrenness. God has not closed His Ears to her cry. He is doing a work in her, and He knows the exact season for her womb to fill up with life. The Scriptures tell us that year after year Hannah went to the house of the Lord and prayed for a son, crying out to God to open her womb. Peninnah would provoke and aggravate her much. She probably boasted about her children, and she may have asked Hannah, "Are you praying for God to give you a son again? How long are you going to continue? You're always going to be barren, why it's been years; don't you think if HaShem were going to open your womb, He would have already done so?" Hannah was more than likely right there at each of Peninnah's births encouraging her to push, wiping her brow, and bathing her newborns.

Beautiful Hannah began to fast and pray and cry out; she was determined. Unfortunately, every year she stayed barren. Each time Peninnah gave birth to a son or daughter, Hannah was there when that precious life came into the world, only to hand the baby to a woman who the Bible says provoked her. She was there watching her husband's eyes light up over his children, his seed. What could she offer him?

How many of you have been crying out to the Father for one thing, repeatedly, year after year, only to come up empty-handed-- only to be provoked by family members and friends who have received their answers? What if HaShem is preparing you for the size of the dream He has shut up in your womb? What if He is preparing your womb for something so glorious and needed for The Body of Messiah that He has to get you ready to receive that seed? What if sorrow goes right in hand with joy?

Hannah wanted a child so severely that she said, Father, if you will bless me with a son, I will give him back to You all the days of his life. The barrenness and the closed-up womb had been in the Father's plan the whole time. He had shut her womb up so tightly that she would have to push and labor in prayer for years to receive. This time of waiting would make her victory worth so much more when it happened. God did not answer her right away. The Father often waits until it is so impossible and the womb looks so dead everyone will know it was only by His Hand. God knew Eli would not be around when his people needed a prophet, priest, and a righteous judge. He knew Eli's sons were wicked. Adonai needed a child who was birthed out of prayer, laid upon the altar, and given to Him at an early age.

Hannah is praying, so engrossed in her need and so empty and filled with anguish that Eli, the priest, thinks she is drunk. But Hannah says, "No, my lord, I am a woman of a sorrowful spirit: I have drunk neither wine nor strong drink, but have poured out my soul before the Lord" (I Samuel 1:15, NASB). Have you been pouring out your soul? Do you look intoxicated by others around you? There was someone else who was called a drunkard. It was none other than the Messiah Yeshua. "The Son of Man came eating and drinking, and they say, 'Behold, a gluttonous man and a drunkard, a friend of tax collectors and sinners!' Yet wisdom is vindicated by her deeds" (Matthew 11:19, NASB).

After great suffering and many requests, Hannah feels the sensations of life in her womb. Precious life that kicks her ribs and claps amid the warm water brings her unspeakable joy. This life in Hannah will have a name and a position of prophet, and multiple Books of the Bible will speak the words of the one in her womb. Samuel is coming forth in just the right season. He is a man whose words never fell to the ground. The name Samuel means, the Lord hears! And He does--He always hears our prayers.

Hannah's story doesn't end here. It is like the widow who had to make a cake for the prophet before she fed her own seed, and in her obedience, a miracle happened. Every day, with that small amount of meal and that dab of oil, it never ran out, just like the manna that rained down from heaven. Every day, the Father showed up. Hannah goes on to have five more children.

> Now Samuel was ministering before the LORD, as a boy wearing a linen ephod. And his mother would make for him a little robe and bring it up to him from year to year when she would come up with her husband to offer the yearly sacrifice. Then Eli would bless Elkanah and his wife, and say, "May the LORD give you children from this woman in place of the one she requested of the LORD." And they went to their own home.
>
> The LORD indeed visited Hannah, and she conceived and gave birth to three sons and two daughters. And the boy Samuel grew up before the LORD.
>
> –I Samuel 2:18-21, NASB

Hannah did not have a one-time experience. She gave her firstborn son to Abba. He gave His firstborn Son to us! Oh, what a blessing to know that Yeshua died for us and that He is the Light of the world. Today if you have been praying for the Father to fill your womb or fill your cupboards, remember He feeds the birds, and He loves you so. Shout with joy over the future. Even if you are gathering sticks and only have a smidgeon of oil in reserves, He sees you. He loves you and is a Father of multiplication.

Part 3

Review

1. Like Joseph waiting in a pit, or the prison, sometimes the testing and time period has to do with how great the assignment is. Can you envision an assignment from heaven for your own life that is bigger than your momentary affliction?

2. If Hannah had requested a pregnancy and immediately became pregnant, how would her story have changed? Would she have given her child to Adonai?

3. Have you ever had to trust God to perform today the same miracle He did yesterday, today?

4. If we could measure the joy of an instant prayer being answered compared to one we've waited for year after year, what greater measure comes from waiting?

5. How is the joy of Adonai our strength?

Blessings

Hopefully, we can begin to probe and search out our times of sorrow and see the manifestation of more significant work at hand. We, like Ruth, make our journey from Moab to the House of Bread, and often we are traveling with bitter weary companions, just as Ruth, who was escorting Naomi back home.

The journey for Ruth was one of uncertainty. It was leaving her family and friends and the familiarity of home for a place she had never been before. Our lives can be filled with twists and turns, potholes, and fender-benders—even fatalities. Misfortunes happen right beside joy. We receive heartbreaking news, like the death of a loved one. Ruth's mother-in-law left Bethlehem with a husband and three sons; she is now returning empty. Naomi keeps telling Ruth to go back to Moab. Naomi does not realize that just around the bend, Ruth is going to get an extreme makeover. Ruth is going to proclaim the God of Abraham, Isaac, and Jacob. Where Naomi goes, Ruth goes. The Father is going to send these two women new beginnings if Naomi will only trust Him.

"Look," said Naomi, "your sister-in-law has gone back to her people and her gods; follow her back home." But Ruth replied: "Do not urge me to leave you or to turn from following you. For wherever you go, I will go, and wherever you live, I will live; your people will be my people, and your God will be my God. Where you die, I will die, and there I will be buried. May the LORD punish me, and ever so severely, if anything but death separates you and me." When Naomi saw that Ruth was determined to go with her, she stopped trying to persuade her.

–Ruth 1:15-18, BSB

Oh, the picture here of selflessness. We have a Body that seems to be ruthless. Where are the Ruths, the ones who will leave family, land, houses, friends, and familiarity, forsaking all to help a grieving bitter widow? What a jewel this woman is. Sometimes we act like Ruth's sister-n-law. We don't want to count the cost.

Naomi does not realize that Ruth has a wealthy landowner waiting for her. Boaz is a representation of the Father. He owns all the lands and all the cattle on all the hills. He notices Ruth and her care for her mother-law. He sees you, even when you feel overlooked and invisible to others.

Ruth takes a journey through a vast desert with a woman when greeted by the town folks, speaks with gall, "Do not call me Naomi; call me Mara, for the Almighty, has dealt very bitterly with me. I went out full, but the LORD has brought me back empty. Why do you call me Naomi, since the LORD has witnessed against me and the Almighty has afflicted me?" (Ruth 1:20-21, NASB). But Naomi, too, will laugh. She, also, will become full of joy. *Naomi* means my sweet delight, and *Ruth* means friend, shepherdess, and one with vision. These two women end up complete and they laugh with joy, but I am getting ahead of myself.

Ruth arrived in Bethlehem as a nameless, faceless foreigner who was tagging along to a strange place with a woman laden with sorrow. Boaz will change all of that. He notices Ruth. Boaz heard of Ruth's courage and her heart to serve. He sees her beauty, and now others see it too. She is a woman of valor-- *Eshet Ḥayil* in Hebrew.

As He did with Ruth, the Father sees you wherever you are right now. Even if the journey is challenging and you have so many unanswered questions like Ruth and Naomi. I surmise they wondered where they would live, how they would provide for themselves. Who would love a Moabite foreigner—two widows? Sometimes things seem so laden with sorrow we cannot see any light. During these seasons we walk towards Bethlehem, the House of Bread and we place one foot in front of the other and wait on our Father to show up.

On the other hand, Orpah, Ruth's sister-in-law, could not get Ruth's assignment. Naomi did not want her to come. They kept telling Ruth to go back to Moab, but once one has tasted Bethlehem and the barley harvest, there is no going back to the gods of Moab. Naomi and Orpah did not know Boaz was waiting for her. They did not understand that her child would be named Obed (servant). Obed would be the father of Jessie, and one day Jessie would have an appointment with a mighty prophet named Samuel, and he would line up all his sons for kingship. His youngest son, David, would get the anointing--the horn of oil poured upon his head, and one day he would be king of all Israel. No, Orpah and Naomi had no idea that kings were coming through Ruth's stained bloodline. The King of Kings was coming.

Maybe you are as heartbroken as Ruth and Naomi. Perhaps life has dealt you much sorrow. Measure it against Naomi, who lost her husband and her sons. I assure you, one day, it will all make sense. One day, joy will bubble up like oil in hot springs. Joy will erupt from that place of suffering, and balm will pour out like rivers of aloes. The Father sees you. He has a plan. It may look different than what you had envisioned, but hold on. He is Boaz, your kinsman Redeemer, and He has your identity. He knows the end of your story.

> Then the women said to Naomi, "Blessed is the LORD who has not left you without a redeemer today and may his name become famous in Israel. 'May he also be to you a restorer of life and a sustainer of your old age; for your daughter-in-law, who loves you and is better to you than

seven sons, has given birth to him.' Then Naomi took the child and laid him in her lap, and became his nurse. The neighbor women gave him a name, saying, 'A son has been born to Naomi!' So they named him Obed. He is the father of Jesse, the father of David."

–Ruth 4:14-17, NASB

Blessings and Shalom,

Tekoa!

Books by Tekoa

The Spirit of Leviathan, Jezebel, and Athaliah is ideal for book clubs and study groups. Each chapter closes with a question review page that causes great personal introspection and is perfect for the season leading up to the fall feasts.

If you think Jezebel is strong, meet the spirit of Athaliah and Leviathan. Job said, "Lay your hand on him (Leviathan); Remember the battle; you will not do it again!" (Job 41:8, NASB).

Many of Adonai's Prophets experienced this thrashing sea serpent. If you or your ministry have been under significant attacks and great difficulties, if your words and deeds have been twisted and people are forming together to destroy you, this book is a must. Can you feel and sense the spirits working through people around you? Do you feel hatred, envy, slander, and a murdering spirit from those who used to honor you? Perhaps even your own family? How does one battle a spirit of such massive strength? Why does Adonai allow this powerful spirit to toss one about like a turbulent tropical storm? What purpose does this testing prove in those like David and Joseph? Tekoa Manning answers these questions and more.

You there! Everyone who thirsts, come to the waters; And you who have no money come, buy and eat. Come, buy wine and milk without money and without cost.
—Isaiah 55:1, NASB

Traveling through a dry, empty desert with rolling tumbleweeds can leave us with cracked lips and an empty spirit. We hunt for water and often find Kool-Aid or a sugar substitute that sounds good and tastes even better, but after a short time, we realize we are still dehydrated and in need of living water. Thirsting for Water is a devotional divided into sections that give the reader the ability to maneuver around from topic to topic, depending on what type of healing or correction is needed for that season. Each section has three different encouraging teachings on circumstances that affect all of us, like struggling with faith, wounds that won't heal, balance, sickness, and love for our enemies.

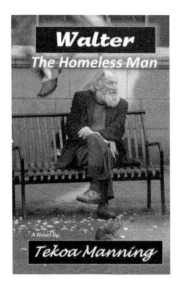

Walter is a man who has suffered great loss and is running from the pain. At night he sleeps under the stars, but during the day, he breaks into a young widow's home for shelter and changes not just her life but every life he touches.

Enjoy this captivating story about loss, integrity, forgiveness, and redemption. This book brings the revelation that, indeed, appearances may be deceiving, and forgiveness can be attainable regardless of the pain. Once you begin on a journey with Walter, you will find yourself forever changed.

Polishing Jade is set in the 1960s in rural Mississippi, where the secrets are as sticky as the jams sold at Taylor's General Store. Jade Gentry is a young girl whose past will not control her future even if it cost her everything. Gripping and suspenseful, Jade will leave you sighing when she sighs, running when she runs, and celebrating when she is triumphant!

Meet an odd cast of characters, including kindly Miss Ellen, a superstitious woman who plants corn in front of her living room window, Renée, a peculiar woman who instinctively knows the deeply hidden secrets of Jade, and a schoolteacher who begins the process of Polishing Jade.

Made in the USA
Middletown, DE
27 February 2022